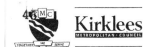

A little bit of magic created with raw wool and a special needle

S I N C O

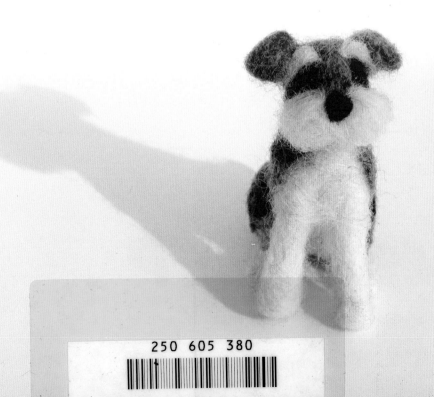

Contents

The Birth of Fleece Dog **04**

Dogs Made of Fleece **05**

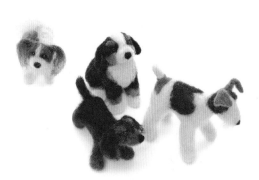

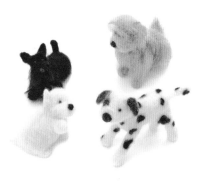

The Birth of Fleece Dog

I make animal topiaries as part of my work. Recently, I have been making lots of dogs with different expressions. It is a pleasure to express the unique characteristics of various breeds in three-dimensional work, because I am a dog-lover in the first place.

One day a friend of mine showed me some sheep's fleece and an intriguing needle. The needle was part of a machine used in a felt factory. I found that by punching a piece of crumpled fleece with this barbed felting needle, I could easily make the fleece into a well-defined ball. I thought I could probably make three-dimensional objects and immediately set out to make a miniature of my dog.

Until then I had worked with moss, the material for topiaries. With the unusual needle and different types of fleece, I could represent the colours and textures of dog hair in a way that was impossible with moss. It opened up possibilities for new pieces of work.

That was only the beginning. Avidly I started making models of one breed of dog after another. I was absorbed in matching the qualities and colours of the fleece with the different types of dog. Having learned that wool and other yarns were suitable for my purpose, I wondered if I could use dog hair. I collected hair from my dog and my friends donated hair from theirs. I kept making models of dogs, using real dog hair. Now there are several dozens of them. Looking at them, I said to myself, "I must put together a book"!

I call the little dogs Fleece Dogs. The word "fleece" may make you think of a soft synthetic fabric, but those who deal in raw wool call sheep's wool "fleece". I got the idea from the word "fleecy" and decided to name the little dogs Fleece Dogs, which is easy to remember.

That was how Fleece Dogs came into being. You can easily make them, using fleece, dog hair, and a magical needle. And here is the book of Fleece Dogs.

Dogs Made of Fleece

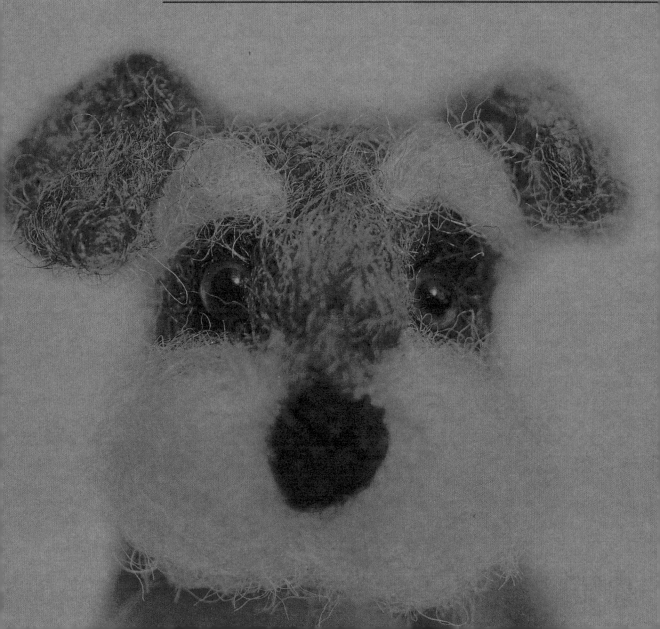

01 Labrador Retriever

Retrievers are very clever dogs, and Labrador Retrievers are especially cheerful and lively. Because of this, they make excellent companions for the family. ➤➤➤p.51/p.58

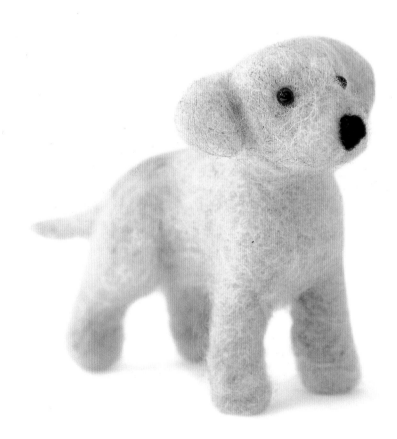

Dachshunds were once used to hunt rabbits because they are active and alert. Miniature Dachshunds are good-natured and are easy to handle because of their small size. They are bred with three types of coat – smooth, long-haired, and wire-haired – and come in several colours. That's why they are so popular. ➡➡p.59

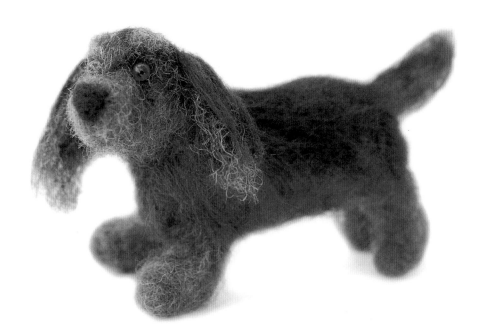

These dogs used to have a reputation for being loyal and affectionate only to their owners, but in fact they are very friendly. ▸▸▸p.60

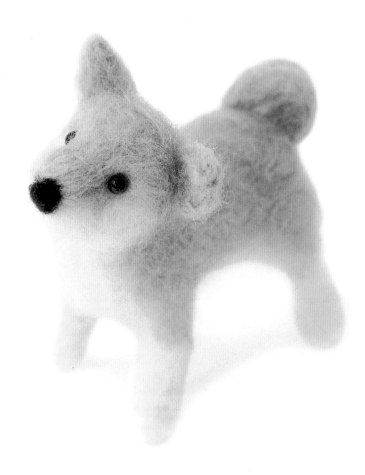

The French Bulldog's distinctive appearance is irresistible. Fashionable people seem to like them. Many of the dogs have a mild temperament – contrary to my expectations. ▸▸▸p.61

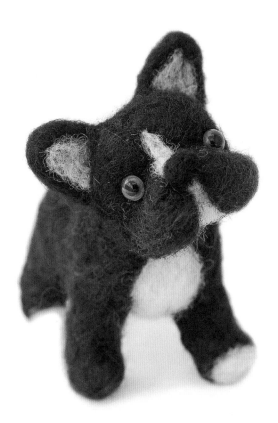

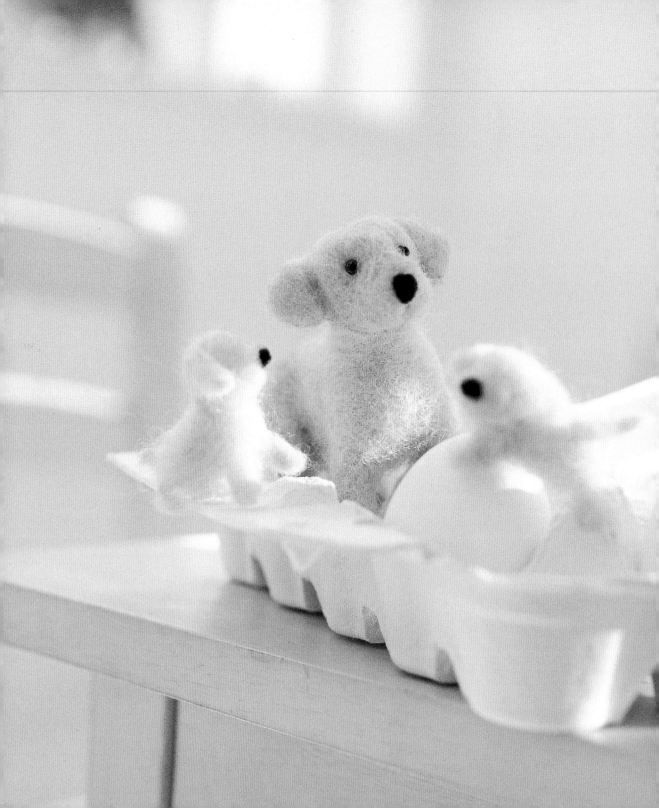

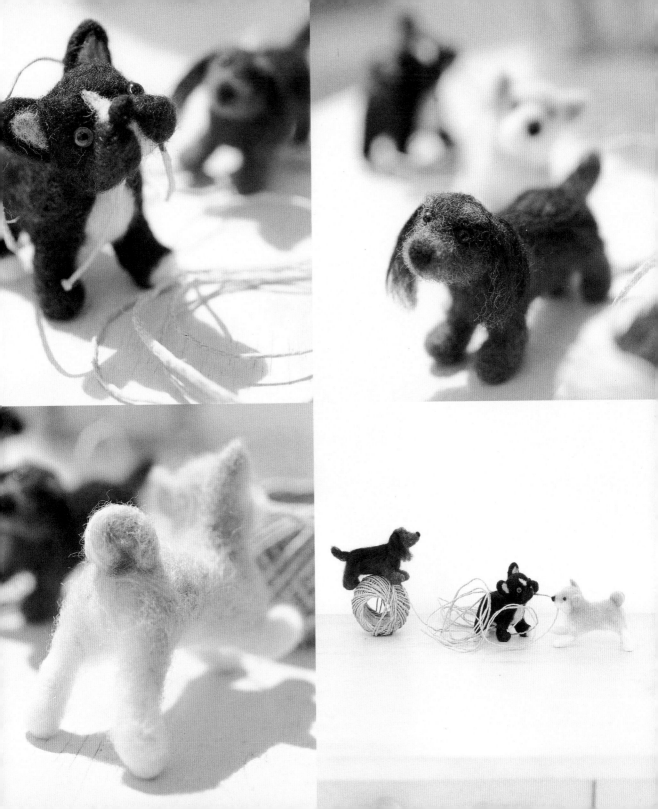

Wirehaired Fox Terriers are quick and agile. Hunters used to use them for fox hunting. They look adorable when they walk in short, quick steps with their fluffy legs. ➡ p.62

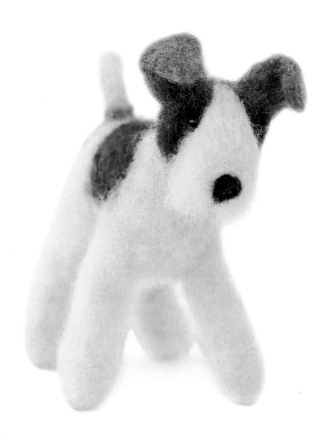

Siberian Huskies have gallant, beautiful features. Their eye colours are striking and the way they walk is cool. Although they may not appear to be very friendly, they are gentle as well as graceful. ➤➤➤p.63

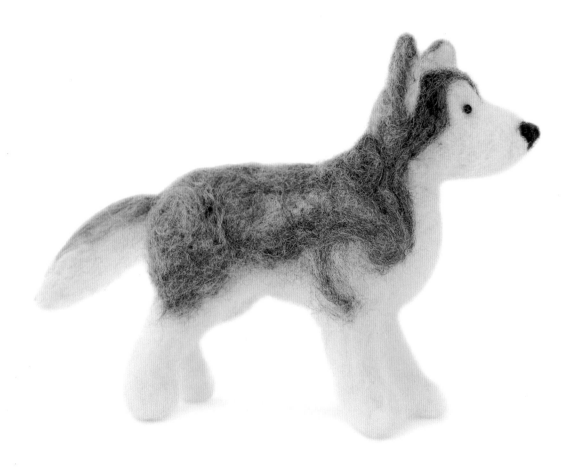

Chihuahuas do wonders for your mind. Their tiny, delicate bodies and their round, dark, moist eyes make you feel very mellow. ➤➤➤p.64

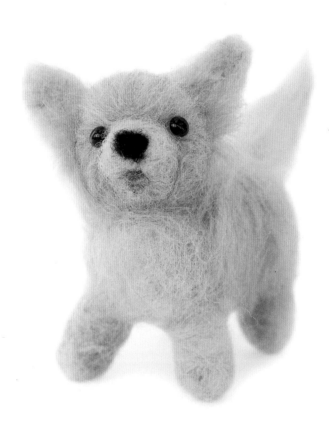

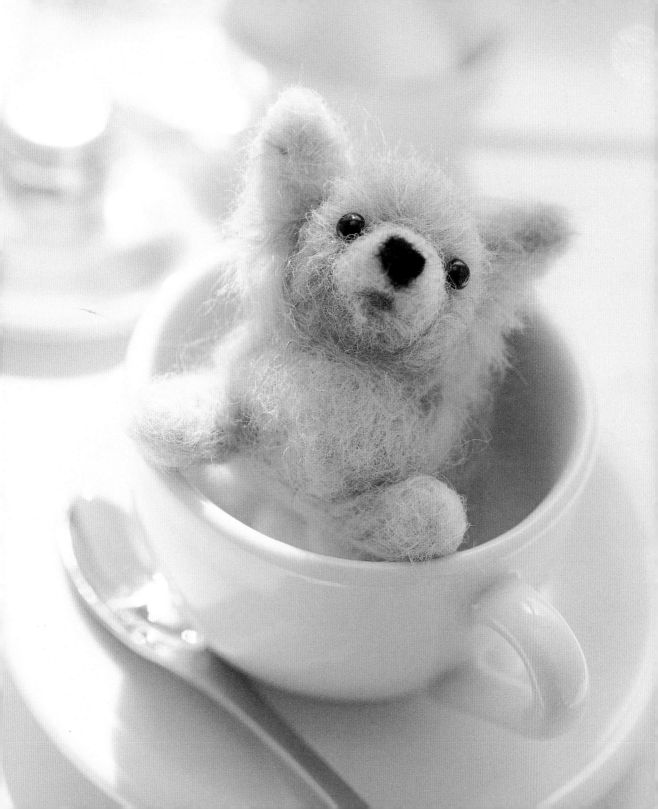

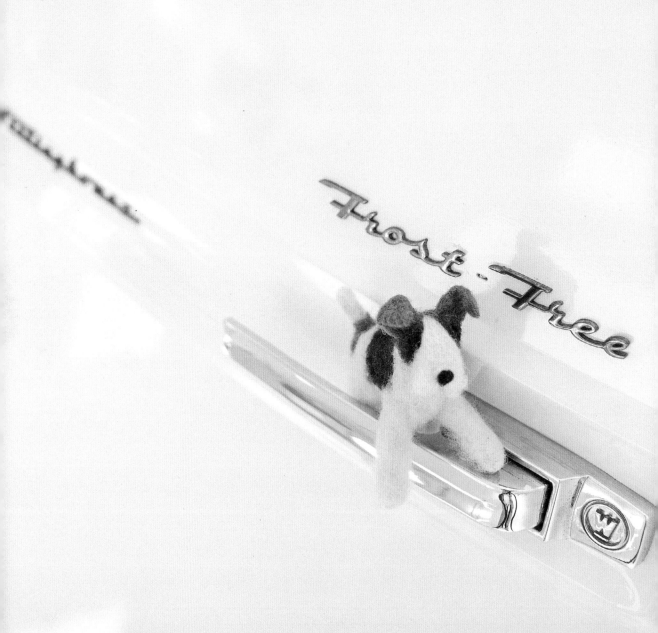

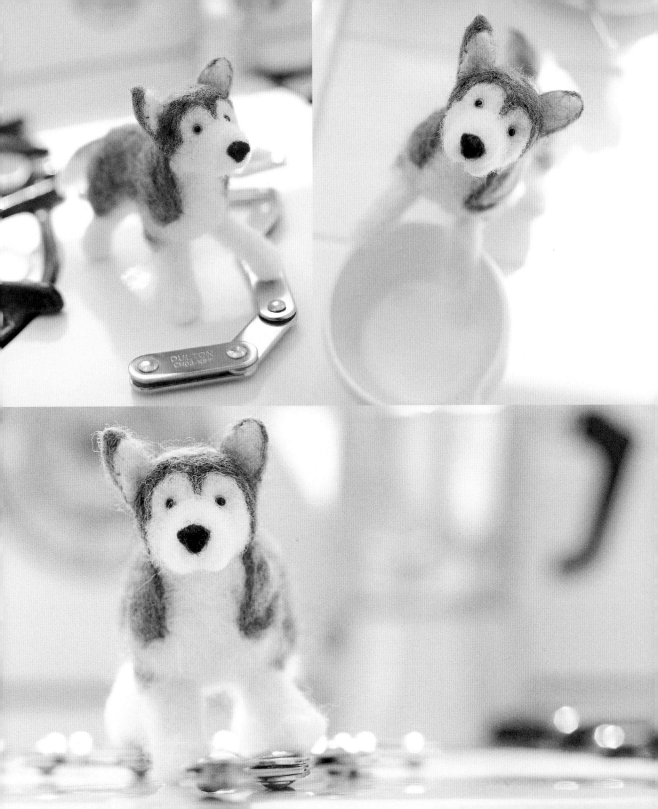

08 | Miniature Schnauzer

This is a very appealing breed. The Schnauzer's tidily trimmed face is so photogenic that I chose this one for the front cover of the book. ➡➡p.65

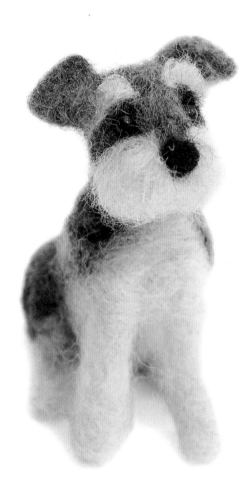

The reddish orange, bushy hair and the large, dark eyes are charming. Pomeranians are small but they make good watchdogs. They are reliable and smart. ➤➤➤p.66

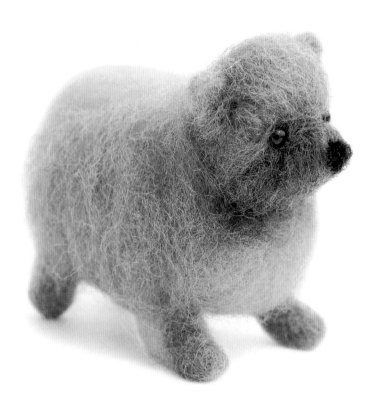

10 | Papillon

 As the name ("butterfly" in French) suggests, Papillons have ears with long hair that look like wings. With a beautiful soft coat, they look graceful when they trot. ➤➤p.67

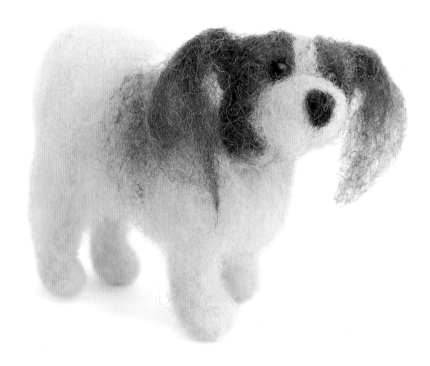

Each Dalmatian has unique black markings – no two Dalmatians look the same. They are good-natured and clever, just like the dogs in the film *101 Dalmatians*. ➼p.68

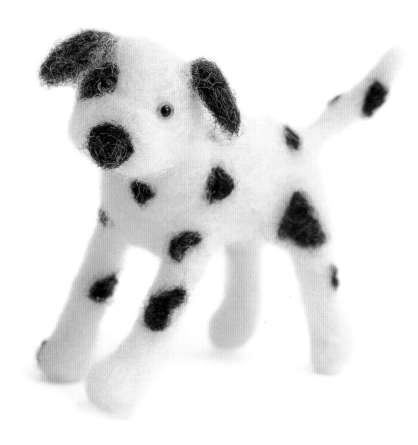

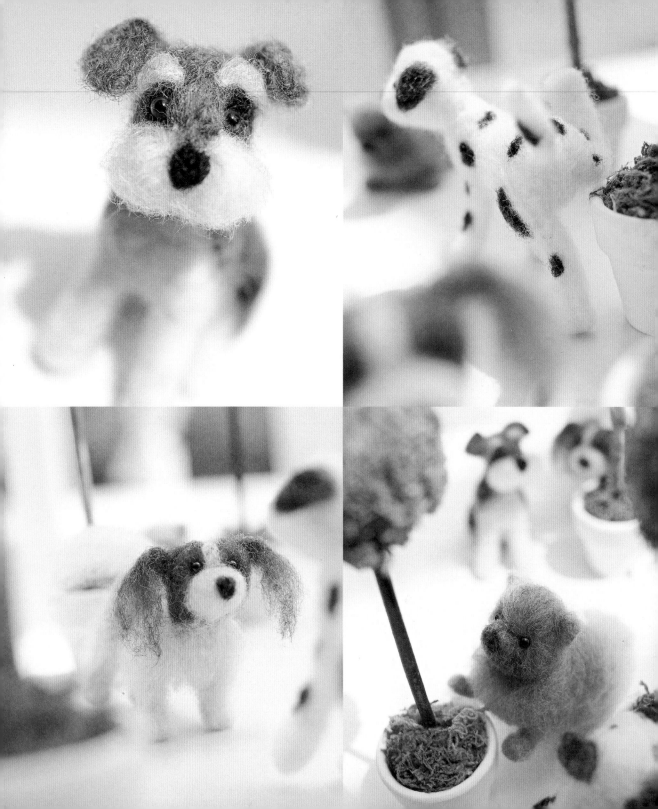

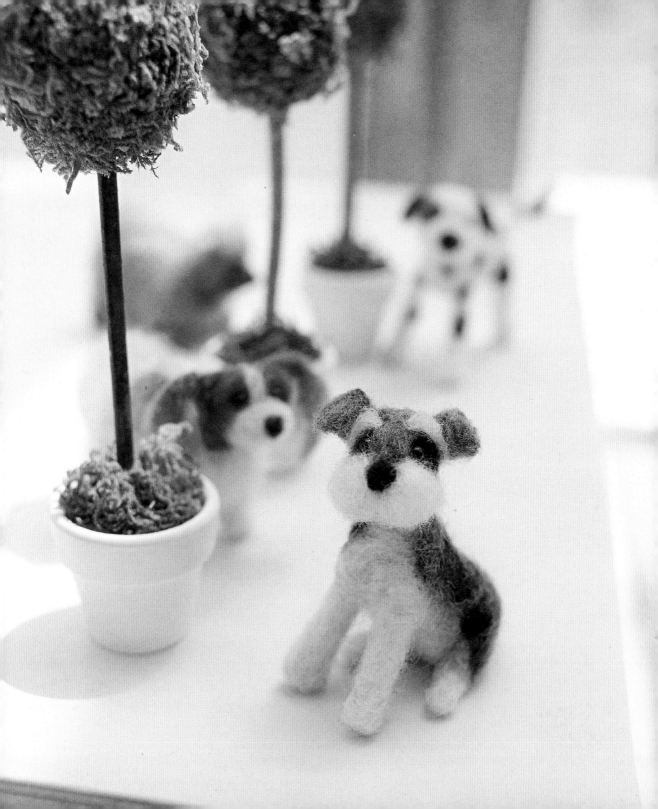

12 | Catalan Sheepdog

Catalan Sheepdogs are popular in Spain, where they are working dogs. I like shaggy faces so much that I just had to make a Catalan Sheepdog. ➡➡p.69

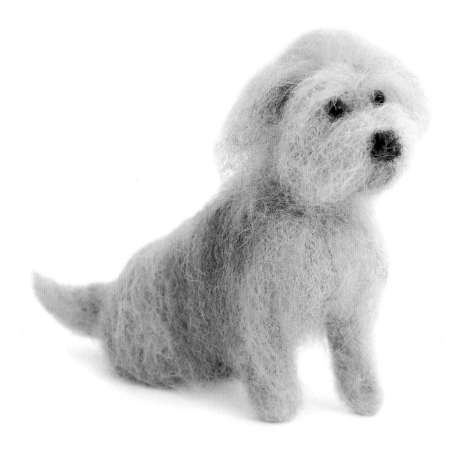

Bernese Mountain Dogs are large and their coats are white, black, and brown. The three colours contrast well with one another. Those who love large dogs find their huge paws, flowing hair, and cute eyebrows irresistible. ●●▶p.70

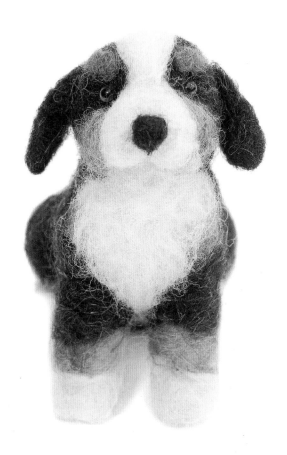

14 | Scottish Terrier

 Scottish Terriers, with jet-black coats and a very distinctive appearance, have been loved for centuries. They are popular among dog fanciers as the most terrier-like terriers. ➤➤➤p.71

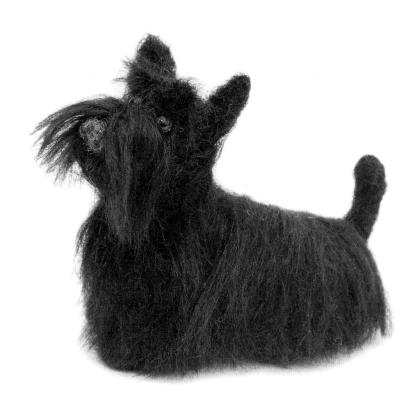

The West Highland White Terrier is very well known. As you can tell from the name, Westies are pure white. With a cute haircut, they could almost be toy dogs. ▶▶▶p.72

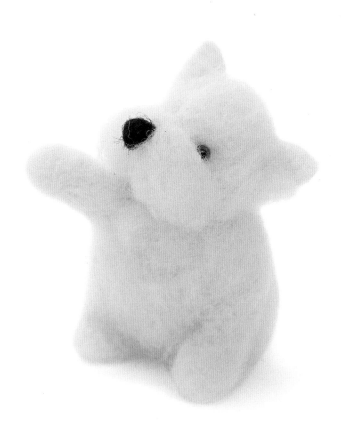

When I see a regal Afghan Hound walking elegantly with his long hair flying in the air, I just have to stop to look at him. It is a beautiful sight. Originally, Afghan Hounds were hunting dogs, so they are said to be fast runners. ➡➡➡p.73

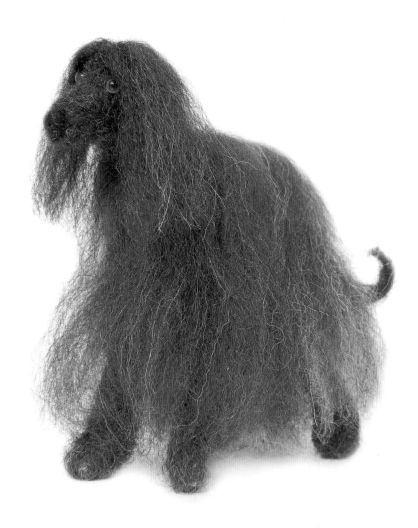

Since the cute "Teddy cut" caught on, Toy Poodles have become very popular.
I made this pooch with a curly fleece that is very similar to a Poodle's wool. ➤➤➤p.74

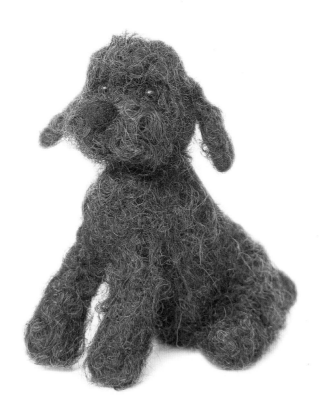

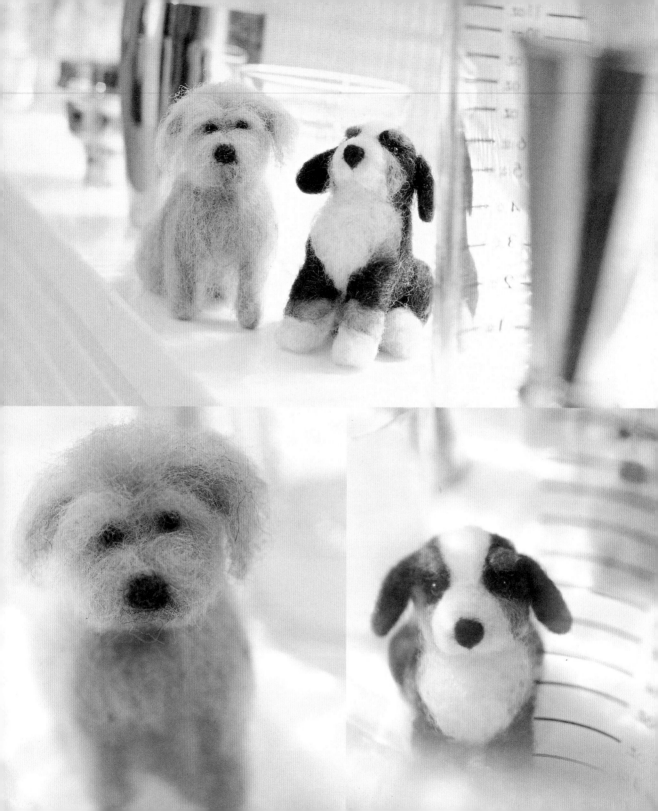

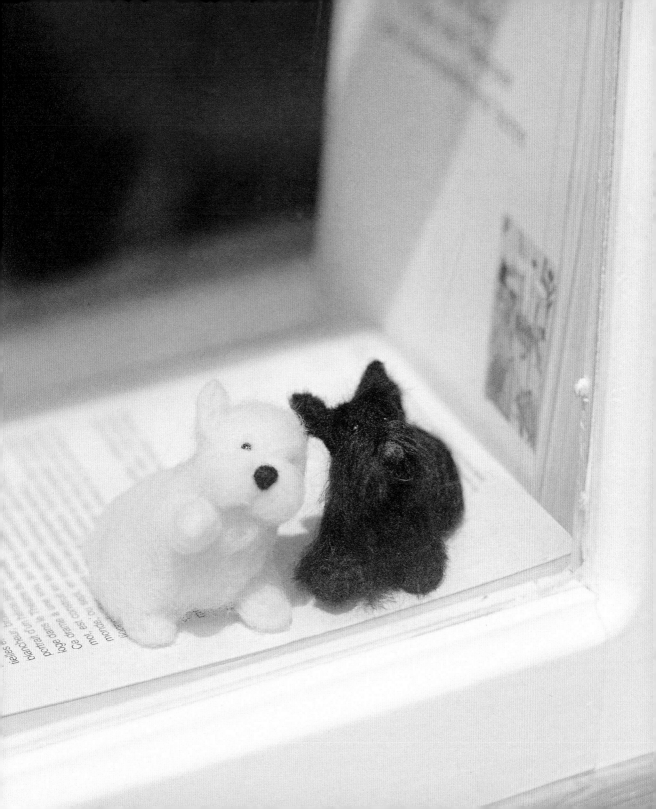

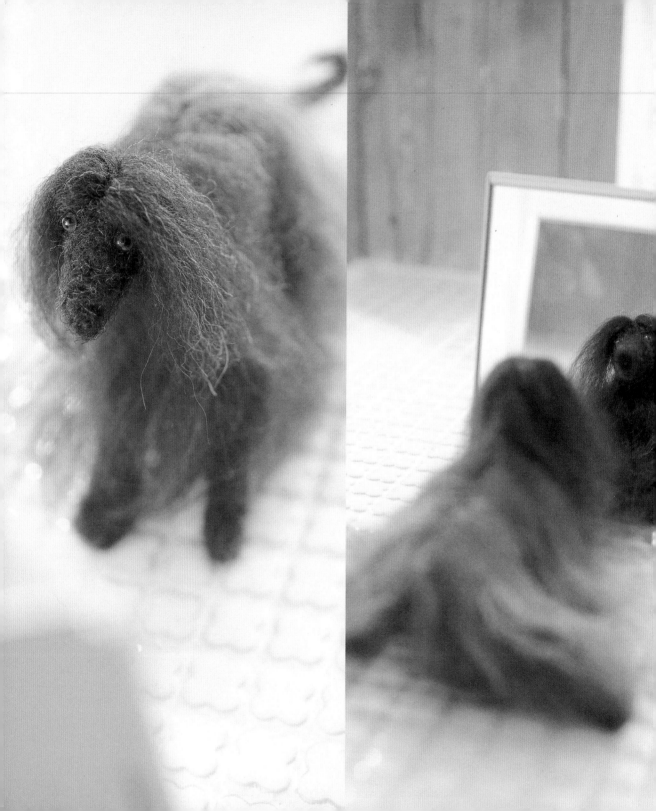

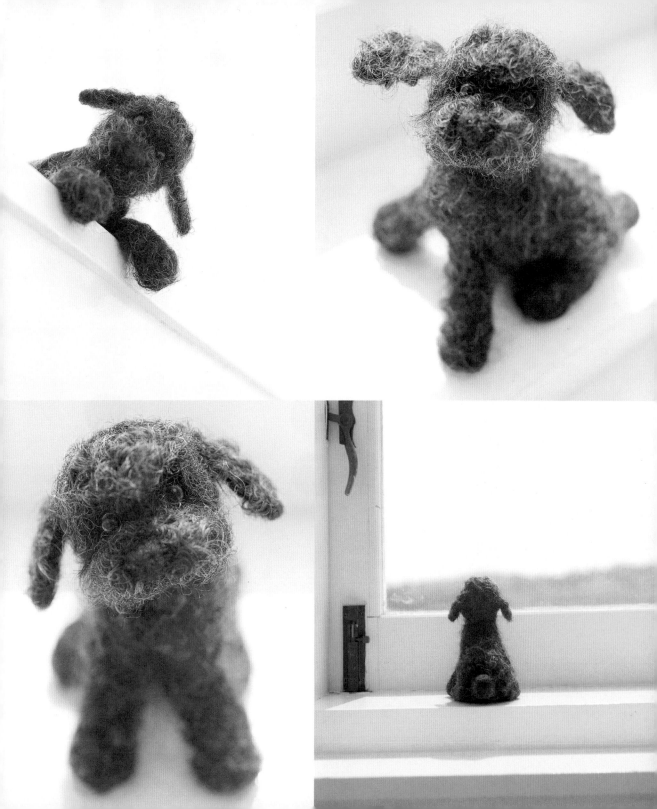

Fleece Colour Chart

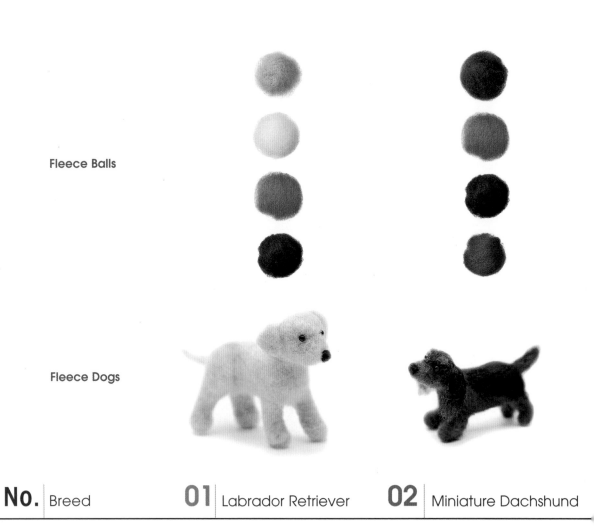

Fleece Balls

Fleece Dogs

No.	Breed	01	Labrador Retriever	02	Miniature Dachshund

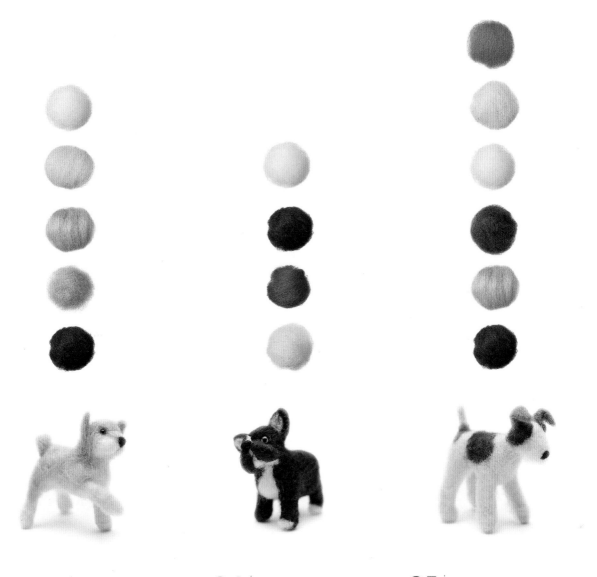

03 | Shiba Inu

04 | French Bulldog

05 | Wirehaired Fox Terrier

Fleece Colour Chart

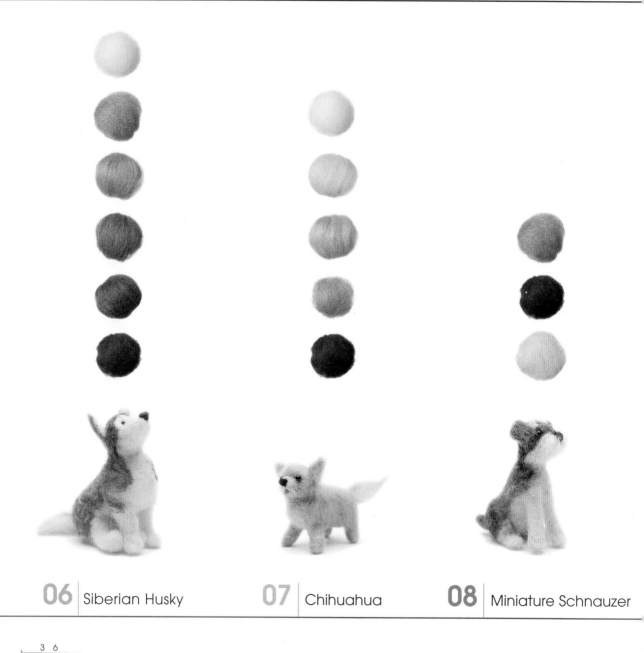

06 Siberian Husky

07 Chihuahua

08 Miniature Schnauzer

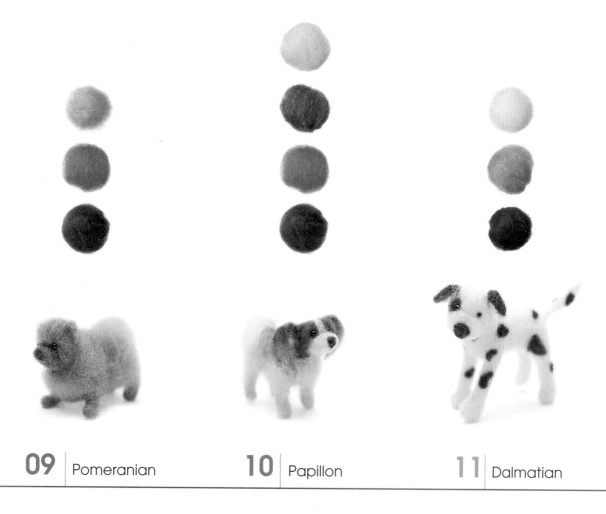

09 | Pomeranian

10 | Papillon

11 | Dalmatian

Fleece Colour Chart

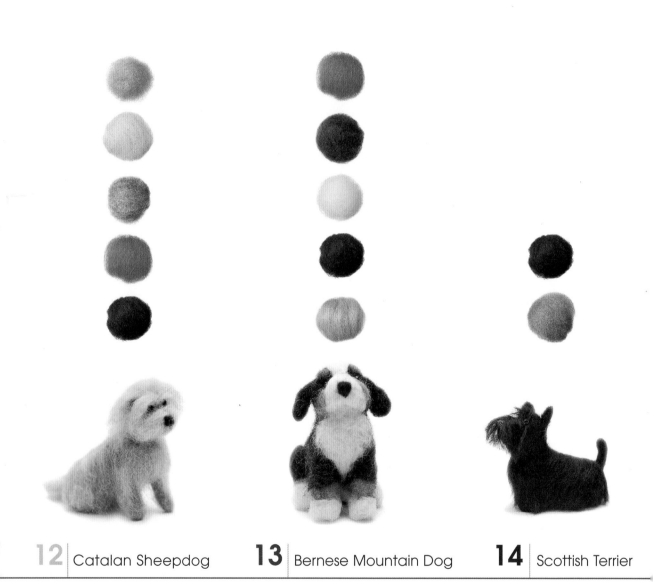

| **12** | Catalan Sheepdog | **13** | Bernese Mountain Dog | **14** | Scottish Terrier |

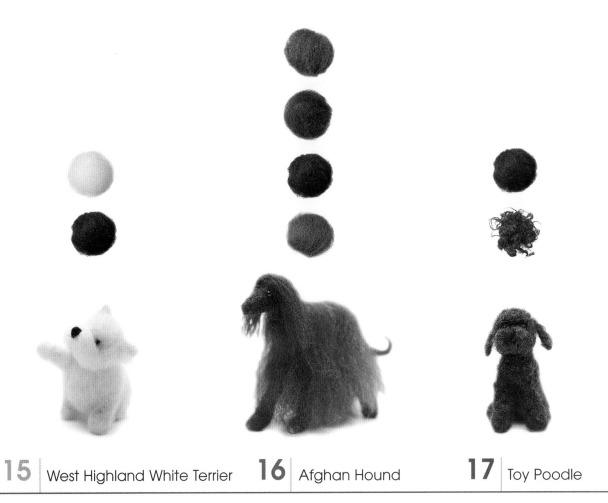

15 | West Highland White Terrier   16 | Afghan Hound   17 | Toy Poodle

Dogs Made of Fleece & Dog Hair

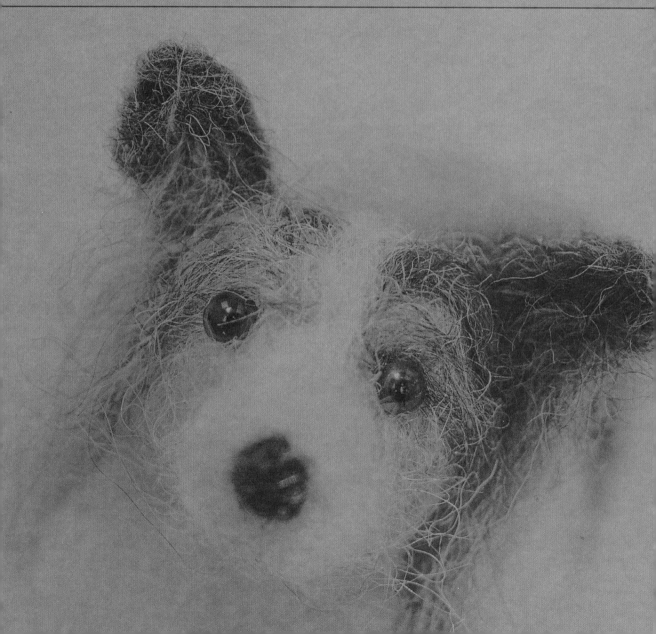

How to Collect Dog Hair

Over the next few pages I will show you how to make a Fleece Dog using dog hair.

From grooming

After you groom your dog, remove the hair from the brush and save it. Put a small amount of dog shampoo in warm water; first soak the hair in it and then wash it. Be careful not to knead the hairs so that it does not become matted and felt-like. It is a good idea to keep the loose hair in something like a clean, used stocking, and wash and dry the hair in that. If you have just shampooed your dog, collect the clean, loose hair from the brush after grooming.

 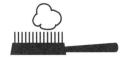 

From trimmings

Using clippings, in addition to the longer hair from grooming, will make your work look more like a real dog. If you have the type of dog that requires trimming, save the clippings.

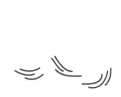 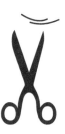 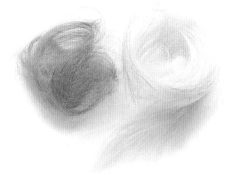

18 | Shetland Sheepdog

A Shetland Sheepdog, also known as a "Sheltie", is a small Collie look-alike. Shelties are intelligent, affectionate, and docile. Miku, my model, is gentle and clever. ➤➤➤p.75

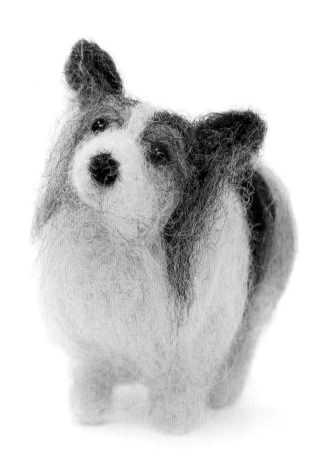

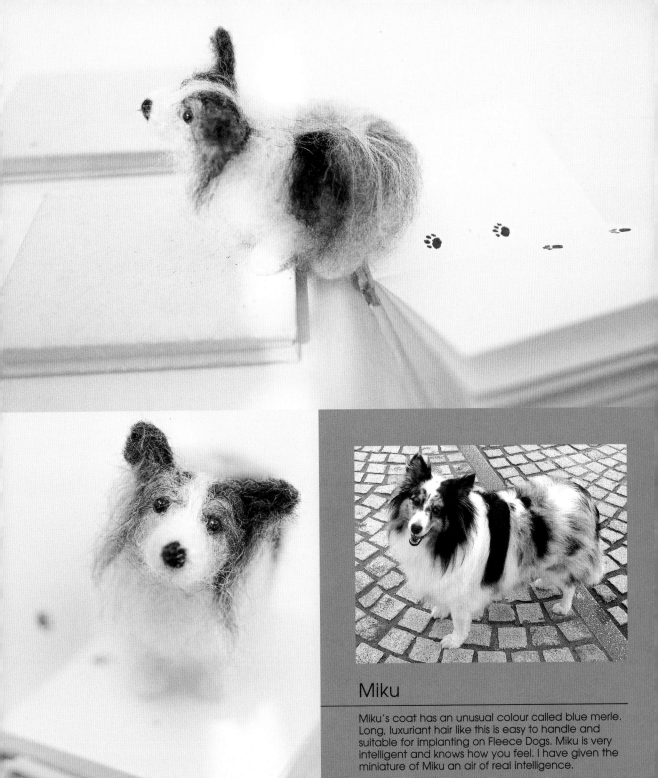

Miku

Miku's coat has an unusual colour called blue merle. Long, luxuriant hair like this is easy to handle and suitable for implanting on Fleece Dogs. Miku is very intelligent and knows how you feel. I have given the miniature of Miku an air of real intelligence.

King Charles I loved this breed of dog. Their beautiful long, silky coats give them an air of nobility. They love being on the laps of people who pay them a lot of attention. Perhaps this is the legacy of being royal dogs. ➤➤➤p.76

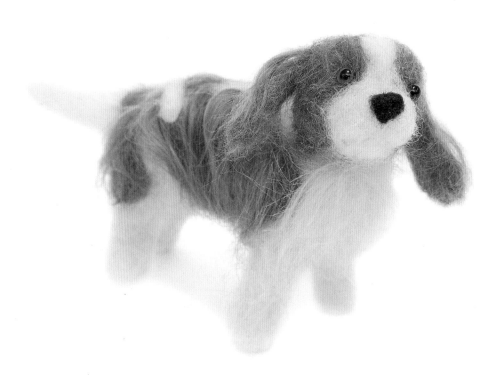

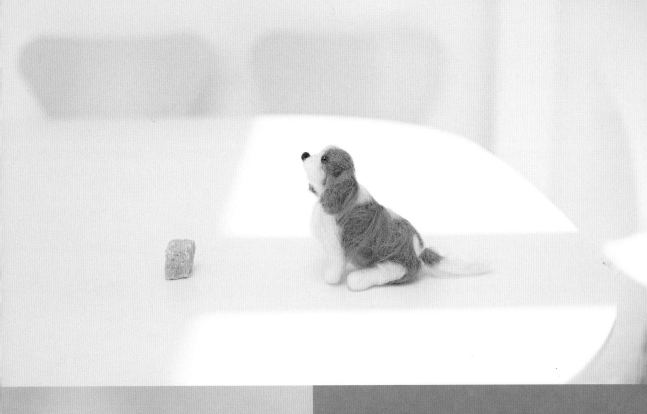

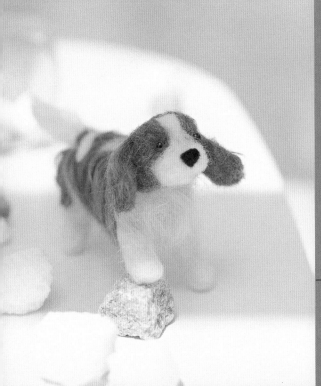

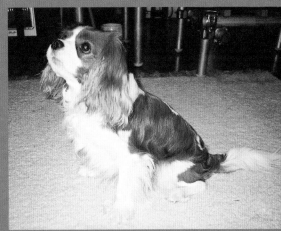

Sucre

Sucre ("sugar" in French) liked playing with a lump of sugar. Unfortunately, she passed away, leaving lots of sweet memories behind. I made this miniature, using her hair, which was collected while she was alive. Her family was very pleased to have the little Sucre.

Petit Basset Griffon Vendeen

We call this breed Petit Basset for short. This agile, short-legged dog was first bred in France for rabbit hunting. A Petit Basset Griffon Vendeen can get along with any dog. With a mop of hair, it looks adorable. ➤➤➤p.77

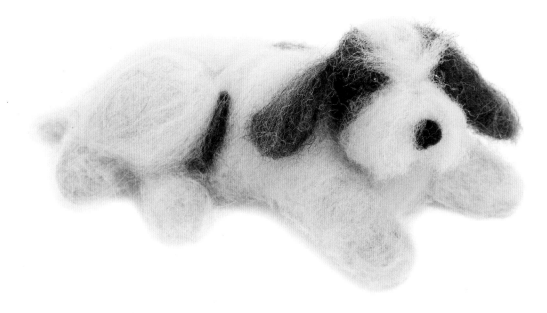

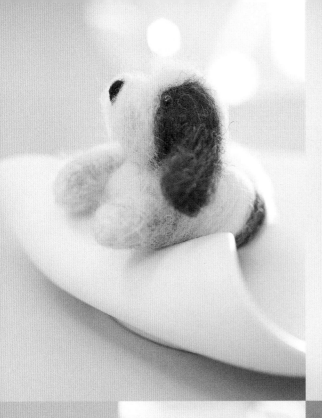

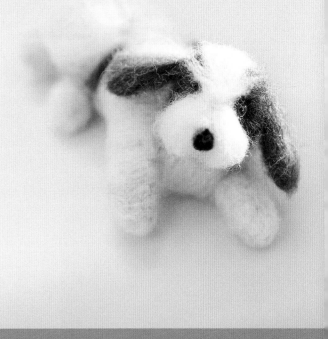

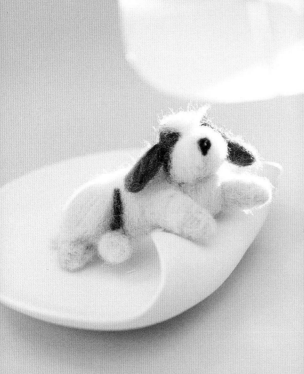

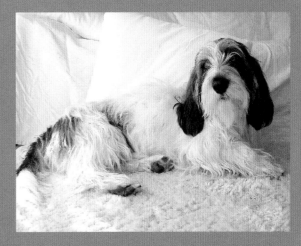

CJ

This is my dog. Because of the quality and length of his hair, I brush him every day. Otherwise, he would look messy. I wash the loose hair and save it. I have already saved quite a bit, so I am thinking of making another, larger, miniature of CJ.

How to Make Fleece Dogs

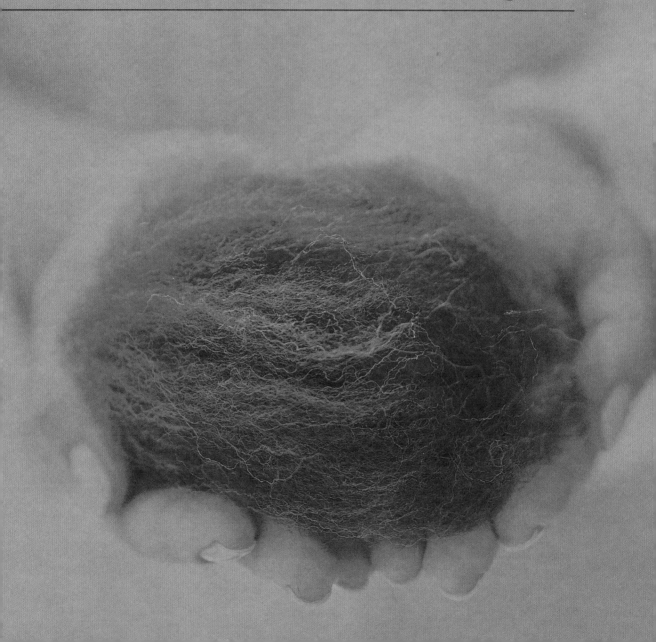

Tools

See p.79 for mail order information.

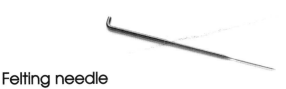

Felting needle

Machines in felt factories use these needles to interlock raw wool. The needle is about 7.5mm (¼in) long and the point has several tiny barbs. The barbs catch and intertwine the fibres. The needles break quite easily, so buy them in multiple packs.

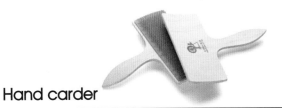

Hand carder

A hand carder looks like a flat brush. If you have two carders, blending fleece will be easy. For instructions on how to use them, see "Mixing the Colours of Fleece" on p.50.

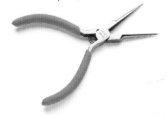

Pliers

You will need pliers when you set the glass eyes in place and if you make wire frames.

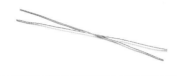

Wire

Use aluminium wire, approximately 1.6mm (½in) in diameter, if you want to make frames for the body and legs. You could use pipe cleaners instead of wire. For instructions, see "How to Make a Frame" on p.78.

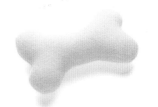

Needle cushion

A needle cushion will keep you from breaking the needle or sticking it into your finger, and protect your work surface. A cushion of fleece with cotton filling would be best, but anything such as a foam pad at least 2.5cm (1in) thick will do, as long as a needle will go straight into it.

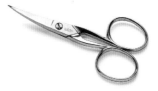

Scissors

Use scissors for trimming to give the finishing touches to your work.

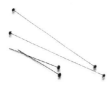

Glass eyes

Glass eyes are handmade and come in different colours, with black pupils. They vary a great deal in size and are attached to pieces of stiff wire or can be attached with thread (see p.61).

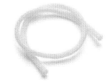

Spindle cord

Tubular, cotton spindle cord is used for belt drives in the textile industry. Put it over the legs of a wire frame (see p.78) or use it as the core for legs (see p.51).

Mixing the Colours of Fleece

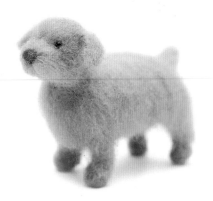

Using fleece in a single colour you may not be able to get the colour or the depth of shade you would like. To show you how to blend fleece I am using the example of a long-haired Golden Retriever, which I made by adapting the basic techniques for making a Labrador Retriever.

Hand carders come in handy for blending a large volume of fleece. If you don't have any carders, try using slicker brushes for dogs, or you could use your fingers. Select small pieces of fleece in different colours and blend them, pulling the fleece with both hands.

01 The Golden Retriever's orangey brown coat is the result of blending four colours (beige, orange, chocolate, and yellow). I used four parts of beige, one part of orange, one part of chocolate, and two parts of yellow. Adjust the mixture while blending it, as necessary.

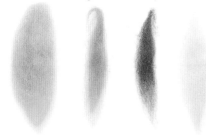

02 Put the fleece on two carders.

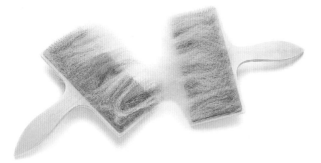

03 Blend the colours of the fleece by combing one carder with the other. Blended well, the colours on both carders will be thoroughly mixed. Blended lightly, the original colours can still be distinguished, randomly distributed. Keep blending until you get the colour you like.

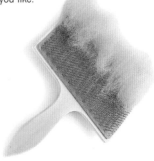

04 To get the right shade for a Golden Retriever, blend the fleece over and over again to make the colour even. When you have finished blending, take the fleece out of the carders.

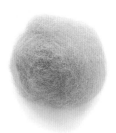

How to Make a Fleece Dog

Let's start with the basics. I would like to give you step-by-step instructions for making a Fleece Dog, using the Labrador Retriever as an example.

I use 1 gram as the basis for measuring fleece for making various parts, although smaller parts require $1/2$ or $1/4$ gram. To give you an idea of quantity, the fleece pictured on page 48 weighs 3 grams. If you don't have any scales, use this as a reference. The amounts of fleece given in this book are based on a rule of thumb. They vary depending on the type of the dog you make – for example, a solid dog is heavier than a fluffy one by approximately 2 grams.

Preparing the fleece

01 You will need 5 to 7 grams of fleece. Blend it in advance, referring to the "Fleece Colour Chart" on p.34 and the instructions on blending. It is a good idea to have a little extra fleece to hand.

Making the legs

02 Make one leg at a time. Cut four lengths of spindle cord to make cores for the legs. Each one should be a little longer than the finished leg (about 5cm (2in) in this example). Spread out $1/4$ gram of fleece and make a strip a little larger than the core. (If you wish to make a wire frame for your dog, refer to p.78.)

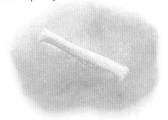

03 From the edge, tightly roll the fleece around the core. Put it on the needle cushion and punch it repeatedly with the needle. Take care not to stab your fingers while doing this.

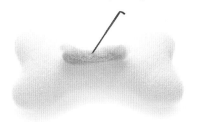

04 Make the paws and main legs solid. The upper ends of the legs will be attached to the body later, so leave them fluffy. Make sure that the four legs are all the same length and thickness.

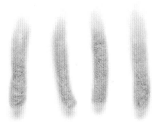

Making the body

05 Make 1 gram of fleece into a long, thin sausage. Roll it up tightly and punch the end of it several times with the needle. This will form the core of the body.

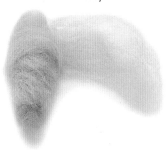

06 Flatten out 1 gram of fleece. Wrap it around the body core and punch it evenly all over with the needle.

Making the head

07 Make 1/2 gram of fleece into a ball and punch it evenly all over with the needle until it gets hard. This will be the core of the head.

08 Keep punching the head core until it gets slightly smaller.

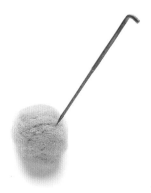

09 Flatten out 1/2 gram of fleece. Wrap it around the head core and punch it evenly all over with the needle.

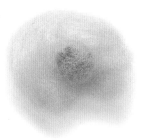

10 Make the head about the size of the ball shown below.

11 From the top of the head, go down about ⅓ of the head length and punch a little harder with the needle to make a straight line across the face and the muzzle.

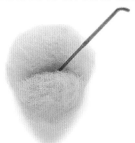

Attaching the legs to the body

12 Attach the fluffy ends of the legs to the body by punching them into position with the needle. If any leg is unstable, add a little fleece to the top and attach it securely to the body. After you have attached the legs, stand the work up on its feet and check the balance. If any leg is too short, add a small amount of fleece to the paw.

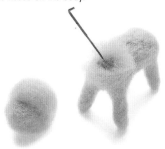

Attaching the head to the body

13 For better results when you attach the head to the body, first put a small amount of fleece onto the neck area of the body. Then put the head on the body and attach the two pieces securely. The idea is to interlock the fleece on the head with the fleece on the body.

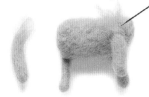

14 After attaching the head to the body, make the neck. Wrap a thin strip of fleece around the neck. Use the needle to pull it up and interlock it with the head.

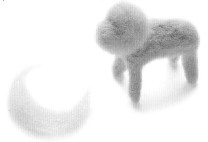

15 When you have made the neck, model the shape and size of the head, paying attention to the proportion of the head to the body.

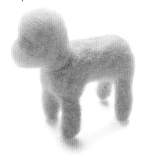

16 Look at the work from the side and check the proportions. Compare it with the actual-size silhouette shown in the instructions on p.58.

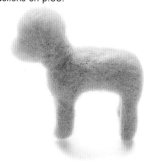

17 Adjust the proportions by adding thin pieces of fleece where necessary. In particular, add more fleece to build up the hips and thighs to give a more dog-like shape.

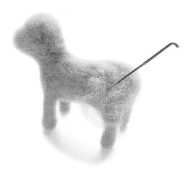

Making the ears

18 For each ear, flatten out a ¼ gram of fleece. Put it on the needle cushion and shape it into an ear, leaving the base end fluffy so that it can be attached to the head. Punch both sides of the ear until the desired shape is achieved.

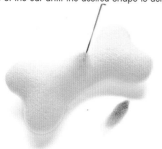

19 Once you have made two ears, fold each in half, and punch along each fold to make a crease.

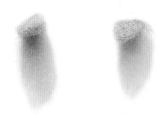

20 With the fluffy ends against the head, position the ears. Punch through the fluffy ends to attach the ears securely.

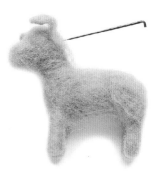

Making the tail

21 Flatten out a ¼ gram of fleece. Place it on the needle cushion and punch it with the needle while carefully rolling it tightly into a tail shape.

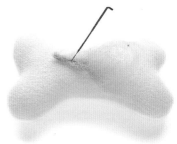

22 Leave one end of the tail fluffy so that it can be attached to the body.

23 Fan out the fluffy part of the tail and wrap it evenly over the dog's rear end. Punch the fleece with the needle to secure the tail in place.

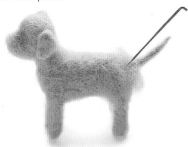

Adding the nose and eyes

24 You need some black fleece for the nose and a pair of glass eyes.

25 Roll the black fleece with your fingertips to make a ball about 5mm (¹/₄in) in diameter for the nose. Attach it to the muzzle and punch it with the needle to adjust the shape.

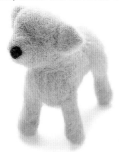

26 Push the glass eyes through the face, aiming them at an angle toward the back of the neck so that the wires cross inside the head. Excess wire will stick out at the back of the head, as shown below, so cut this off. Pull the wires so that they are tight and then bend the ends into a "U" shape.

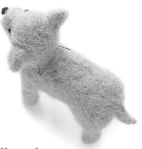

Finishing the dog

27 Look at your dog from the side and check its proportions. Compare it with the actual-size silhouette shown on p.58.

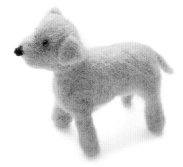

28 The dog will look more realistic if you add a small amount of reddish brown fleece to its muzzle, the tips of its ears, and its rear end (see p.58).

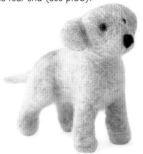

Additional Techniques

Here are some techniques for making each breed more lifelike.

Implanting hair

01   Implant long hair in two or three stages, starting on each side of the abdomen and working upward. Take some fleece and, without arranging the shape, fold it in two. Attach the folded end to the body, punching it with the needle.

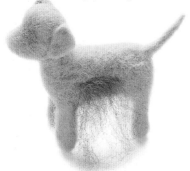

02   Repeat the first step once or twice more, depending on the length of the legs and the amount of hair you need. When complete, trim the length and shape of the hair.

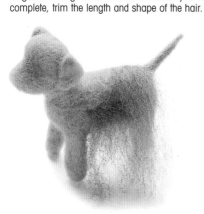

Adding markings

01   Select fleece in the appropriate colour for the markings and put it on the body. Punch it with the needle while arranging the shape. Take care to keep your fingers out of the way of the needle.

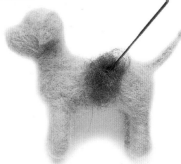

02   If you want to make a distinctive marking, add a substantial amount of extra fleece. If you are just adding a subtle gradation, use a thin layer of fleece and adjust the shade while working on it.

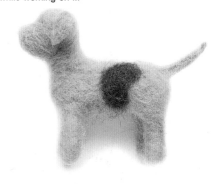

How to Make Each Dog

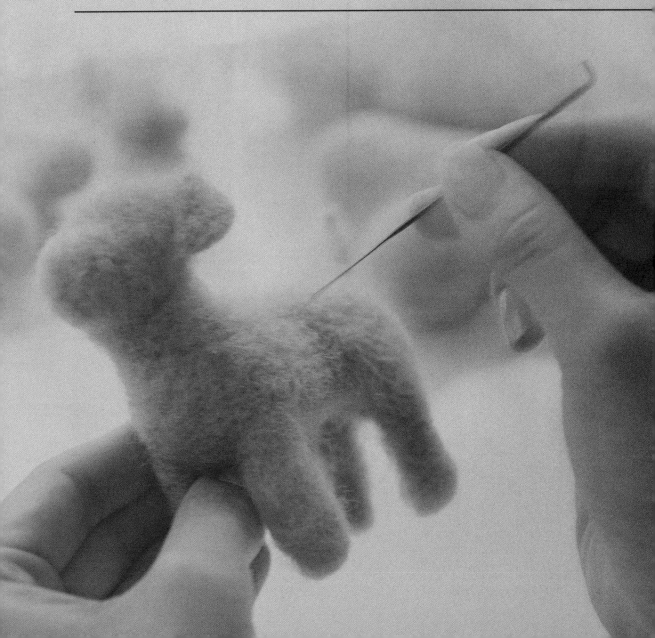

01 | Labrador Retriever

fleece: Romney (white, beige, reddish brown), merino (black)
weight: approx. 7 grams
glass eyes: 3mm (1/8in), medium brown

▸▸▸p.06/p.34/p.51

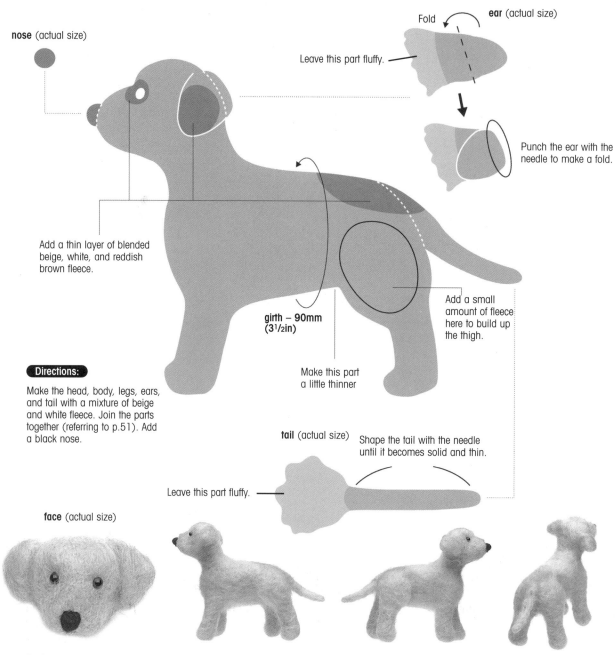

nose (actual size)

ear (actual size)

Fold

Leave this part fluffy.

Punch the ear with the needle to make a fold.

Add a thin layer of blended beige, white, and reddish brown fleece.

Add a small amount of fleece here to build up the thigh.

girth – 90mm (3¹/₂in)

Make this part a little thinner

Directions:

Make the head, body, legs, ears, and tail with a mixture of beige and white fleece. Join the parts together (referring to p.51). Add a black nose.

tail (actual size)

Shape the tail with the needle until it becomes solid and thin.

Leave this part fluffy.

face (actual size)

➡➡➡ p.07/p.34

fleece: Romney (chocolate, reddish brown, black), merino (black, dark brown)
weight: approx. 5 grams
glass eyes: 3mm (1/8in), medium brown

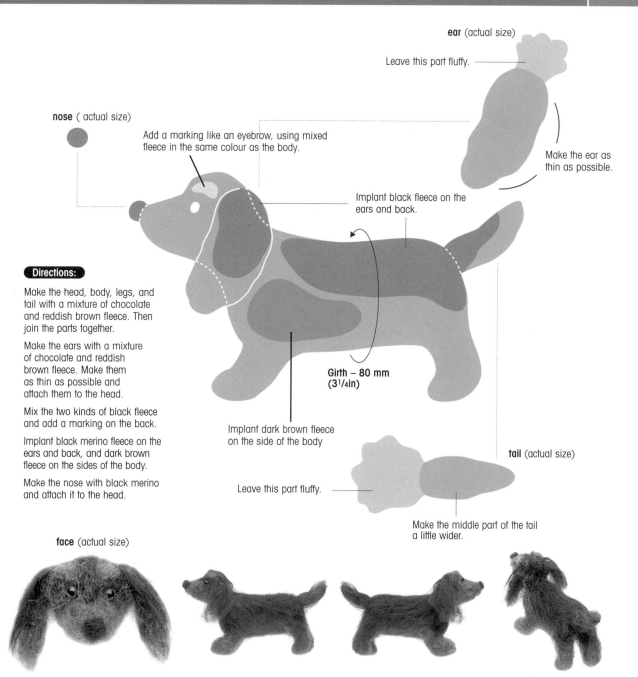

ear (actual size)

Leave this part fluffy. ——

nose (actual size)

Add a marking like an eyebrow, using mixed fleece in the same colour as the body.

Make the ear as thin as possible.

Implant black fleece on the ears and back.

Directions:

Make the head, body, legs, and tail with a mixture of chocolate and reddish brown fleece. Then join the parts together.

Make the ears with a mixture of chocolate and reddish brown fleece. Make them as thin as possible and attach them to the head.

Mix the two kinds of black fleece and add a marking on the back.

Implant black merino fleece on the ears and back, and dark brown fleece on the sides of the body.

Make the nose with black merino and attach it to the head.

Girth – 80 mm (3¹/₄in)

Implant dark brown fleece on the side of the body

tail (actual size)

Leave this part fluffy. ——

Make the middle part of the tail a little wider.

face (actual size)

fleece: Romney (white, beige), merino (black, light beige), alpaca (beige)
weight: approx. 6 grams
glass eyes: 3mm (¹/₈in), medium brown

▶▶▶p.08/p.35

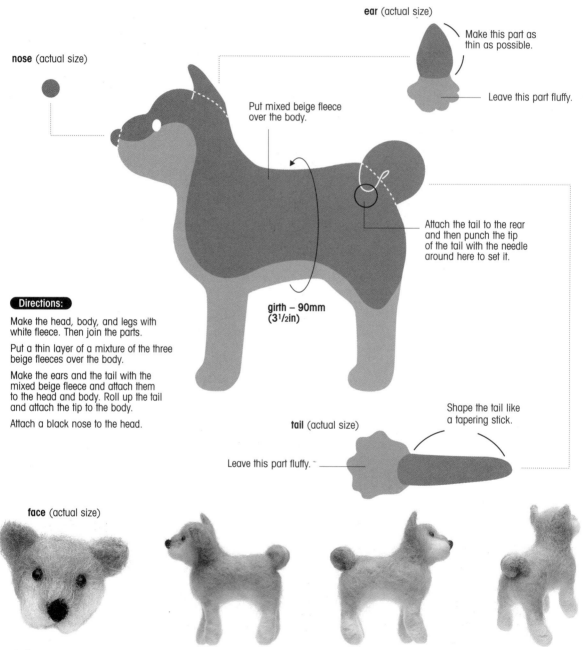

nose (actual size)

ear (actual size)

Make this part as thin as possible.

Leave this part fluffy.

Put mixed beige fleece over the body.

Attach the tail to the rear and then punch the tip of the tail with the needle around here to set it.

girth – 90mm (3¹/₂in)

Directions:

Make the head, body, and legs with white fleece. Then join the parts.

Put a thin layer of a mixture of the three beige fleeces over the body.

Make the ears and the tail with the mixed beige fleece and attach them to the head and body. Roll up the tail and attach the tip to the body.

Attach a black nose to the head.

Shape the tail like a tapering stick.

tail (actual size)

Leave this part fluffy.

face (actual size)

➤➤➤p.09/p.35

fleece: Romney (white, black, pale pink), merino (black, dark brown)
weight: approx. 6 grams
glass eyes: 4mm (³/₁₆in), clear

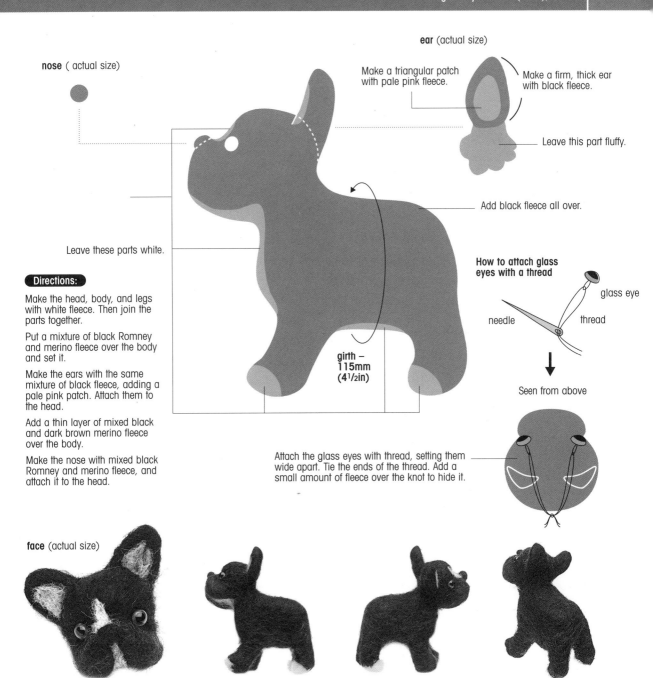

nose (actual size)

ear (actual size)

Make a triangular patch with pale pink fleece.

Make a firm, thick ear with black fleece.

Leave this part fluffy.

Add black fleece all over.

Leave these parts white.

How to attach glass eyes with a thread

glass eye

needle   thread

Seen from above

girth – 115mm (4¹/₂in)

Directions:

Make the head, body, and legs with white fleece. Then join the parts together.

Put a mixture of black Romney and merino fleece over the body and set it.

Make the ears with the same mixture of black fleece, adding a pale pink patch. Attach them to the head.

Add a thin layer of mixed black and dark brown merino fleece over the body.

Make the nose with mixed black Romney and merino fleece, and attach it to the head.

Attach the glass eyes with thread, setting them wide apart. Tie the ends of the thread. Add a small amount of fleece over the knot to hide it.

face (actual size)

fleece: Romney (white, light grey, reddish brown, chocolate, black), merino (black, light beige)
weight: approx. 7 grams
glass eyes: 3mm (¹/₈in), medium brown

➤➤➤p.12/p.35

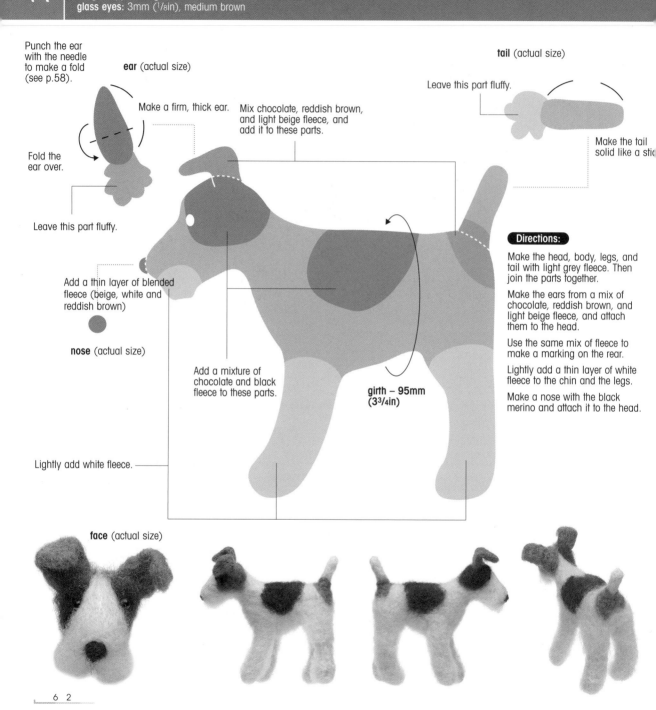

Punch the ear with the needle to make a fold (see p.58).

ear (actual size)

Make a firm, thick ear.

Fold the ear over.

Leave this part fluffy.

Mix chocolate, reddish brown, and light beige fleece, and add it to these parts.

tail (actual size)

Leave this part fluffy.

Make the tail solid like a stick

Add a thin layer of blended fleece (beige, white and reddish brown)

nose (actual size)

Add a mixture of chocolate and black fleece to these parts.

girth – 95mm (3³/₄in)

Lightly add white fleece.

Directions:

Make the head, body, legs, and tail with light grey fleece. Then join the parts together.

Make the ears from a mix of chocolate, reddish brown, and light beige fleece, and attach them to the head.

Use the same mix of fleece to make a marking on the rear.

Lightly add a thin layer of white fleece to the chin and the legs.

Make a nose with the black merino and attach it to the head.

face (actual size)

---►p.13/p.36

fleece: Romney (white, grey), merino (black, medium grey, light grey, dark grey)
weight: approx. 8 grams
glass eyes: 3mm (1/8in), blue

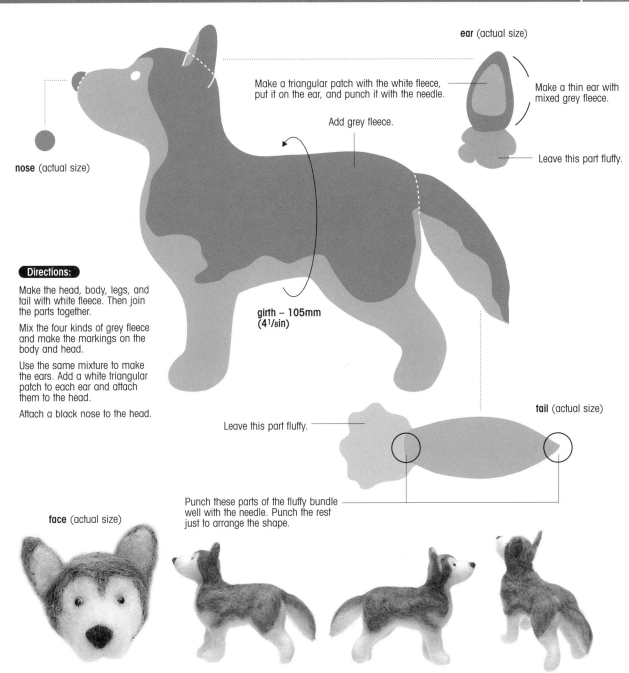

ear (actual size)

Make a triangular patch with the white fleece, put it on the ear, and punch it with the needle.

Make a thin ear with mixed grey fleece.

Add grey fleece.

Leave this part fluffy.

nose (actual size)

Directions:

Make the head, body, legs, and tail with white fleece. Then join the parts together.

Mix the four kinds of grey fleece and make the markings on the body and head.

Use the same mixture to make the ears. Add a white triangular patch to each ear and attach them to the head.

Attach a black nose to the head.

girth – 105mm (4¹/₈in)

tail (actual size)

Leave this part fluffy.

Punch these parts of the fluffy bundle well with the needle. Punch the rest just to arrange the shape.

face (actual size)

fleece: Romney (white, pink), merino (black, light beige), alpaca (beige)
weight: approx. 5 grams
glass eyes: 4mm (³/₁₆in), black

➤➤➤ p.14/p.36

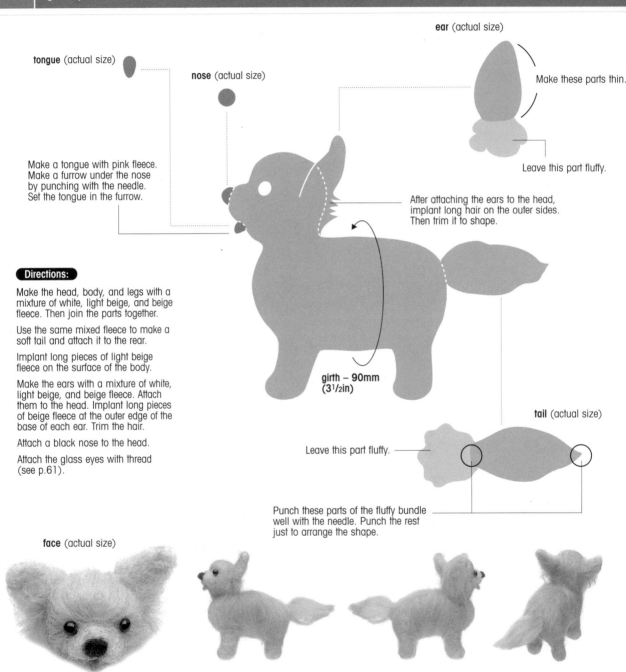

tongue (actual size)

nose (actual size)

ear (actual size)

Make these parts thin.

Leave this part fluffy.

Make a tongue with pink fleece.
Make a furrow under the nose
by punching with the needle.
Set the tongue in the furrow.

After attaching the ears to the head,
implant long hair on the outer sides.
Then trim it to shape.

Directions:

Make the head, body, and legs with a
mixture of white, light beige, and beige
fleece. Then join the parts together.

Use the same mixed fleece to make a
soft tail and attach it to the rear.

Implant long pieces of light beige
fleece on the surface of the body.

Make the ears with a mixture of white,
light beige, and beige fleece. Attach
them to the head. Implant long pieces
of beige fleece at the outer edge of the
base of each ear. Trim the hair.

Attach a black nose to the head.

Attach the glass eyes with thread
(see p.61).

girth – 90mm
(3¹/₂in)

tail (actual size)

Leave this part fluffy.

Punch these parts of the fluffy bundle
well with the needle. Punch the rest
just to arrange the shape.

face (actual size)

p.18/p.36

fleece: Romney (light grey, grey, black), merino (black)
weight: approx. 6 grams
glass eyes: 3mm (1/8in), medium brown

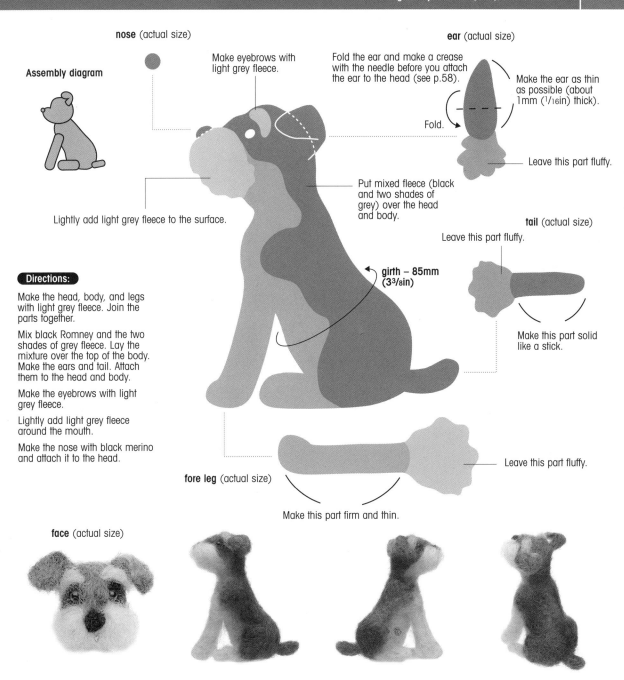

nose (actual size)

Assembly diagram

Make eyebrows with light grey fleece.

ear (actual size)

Fold the ear and make a crease with the needle before you attach the ear to the head (see p.58).

Make the ear as thin as possible (about 1mm (1/16in) thick).

Fold.

Leave this part fluffy.

Lightly add light grey fleece to the surface.

Put mixed fleece (black and two shades of grey) over the head and body.

tail (actual size)

Leave this part fluffy.

girth – 85mm (3 3/8in)

Make this part solid like a stick.

Directions:

Make the head, body, and legs with light grey fleece. Join the parts together.

Mix black Romney and the two shades of grey fleece. Lay the mixture over the top of the body. Make the ears and tail. Attach them to the head and body.

Make the eyebrows with light grey fleece.

Lightly add light grey fleece around the mouth.

Make the nose with black merino and attach it to the head.

Leave this part fluffy.

fore leg (actual size)

Make this part firm and thin.

face (actual size)

fleece: Romney (beige, chocolate, reddish brown)
weight: approx. 5.5 grams
glass eyes: 3mm (1/8in), medium brown

►►► p.19/p.37

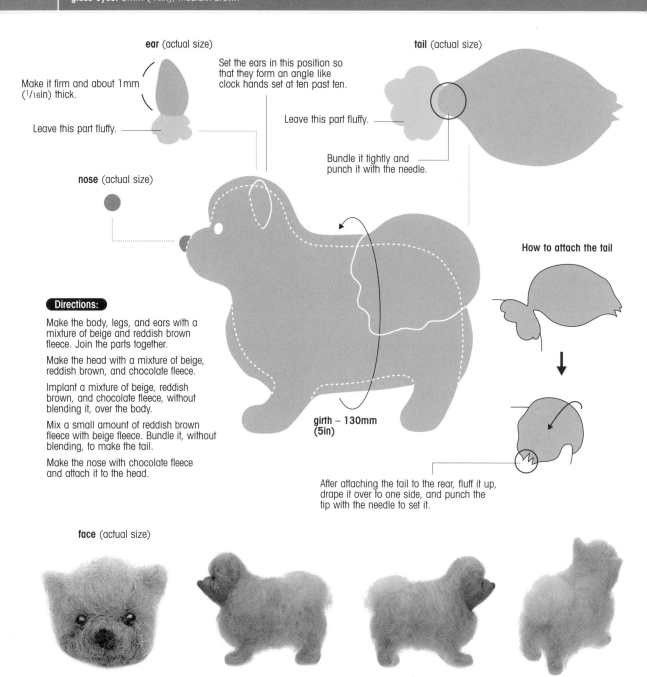

ear (actual size)

Make it firm and about 1mm (1/16in) thick.

Leave this part fluffy.

Set the ears in this position so that they form an angle like clock hands set at ten past ten.

tail (actual size)

Leave this part fluffy.

Bundle it tightly and punch it with the needle.

nose (actual size)

How to attach the tail

Directions:

Make the body, legs, and ears with a mixture of beige and reddish brown fleece. Join the parts together.

Make the head with a mixture of beige, reddish brown, and chocolate fleece.

Implant a mixture of beige, reddish brown, and chocolate fleece, without blending it, over the body.

Mix a small amount of reddish brown fleece with beige fleece. Bundle it, without blending, to make the tail.

Make the nose with chocolate fleece and attach it to the head.

girth – 130mm (5in)

After attaching the tail to the rear, fluff it up, drape it over to one side, and punch the tip with the needle to set it.

face (actual size)

►►►p.20/p.37

fleece: Romney (light grey, brown, chocolate, reddish brown), merino (black, dark brown)
weight: approx. 5 grams
glass eyes: 3mm (1/8in), medium brown

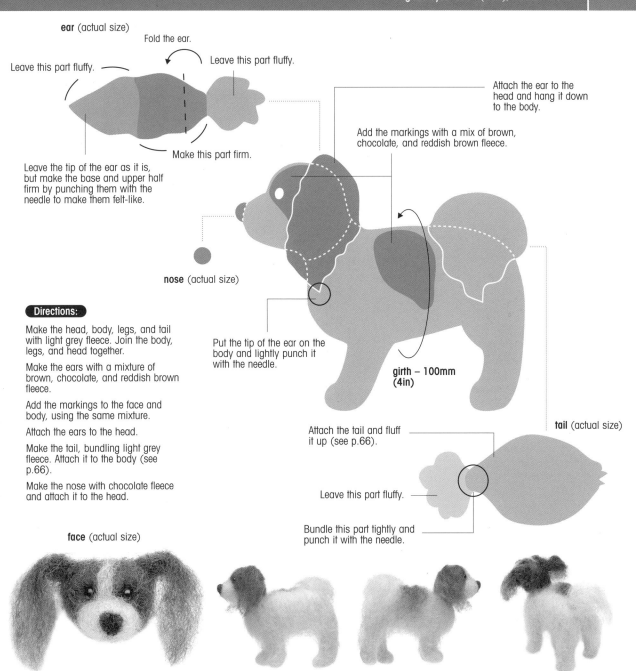

ear (actual size)

Fold the ear.

Leave this part fluffy.

Leave this part fluffy.

Leave the tip of the ear as it is, but make the base and upper half firm by punching them with the needle to make them felt-like.

Make this part firm.

Attach the ear to the head and hang it down to the body.

Add the markings with a mix of brown, chocolate, and reddish brown fleece.

nose (actual size)

Directions:

Make the head, body, legs, and tail with light grey fleece. Join the body, legs, and head together.

Make the ears with a mixture of brown, chocolate, and reddish brown fleece.

Add the markings to the face and body, using the same mixture.

Attach the ears to the head.

Make the tail, bundling light grey fleece. Attach it to the body (see p.66).

Make the nose with chocolate fleece and attach it to the head.

Put the tip of the ear on the body and lightly punch it with the needle.

girth – 100mm (4in)

Attach the tail and fluff it up (see p.66).

tail (actual size)

Leave this part fluffy.

Bundle this part tightly and punch it with the needle.

face (actual size)

fleece: Romney (white, grey, black)
weight: approx. 6 grams
glass eyes: 3mm (1/8in), blue

▶▶▶p.21/p.37

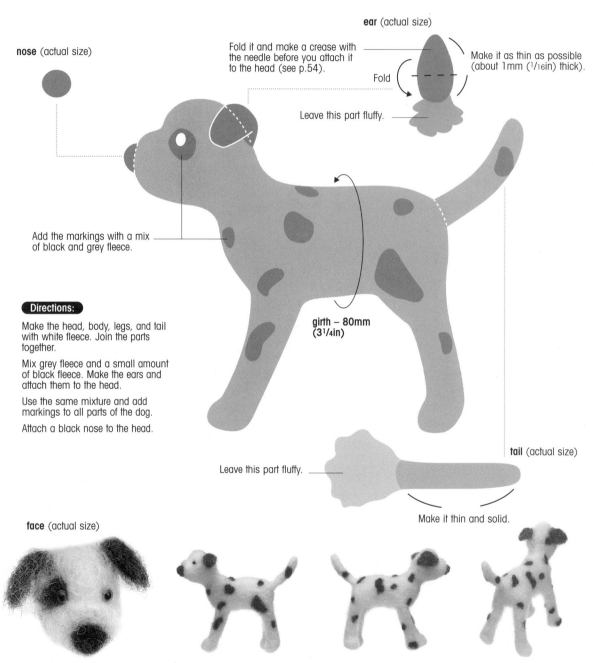

nose (actual size)

ear (actual size)

Fold it and make a crease with the needle before you attach it to the head (see p.54).

Make it as thin as possible (about 1mm (1/16in) thick).

Fold

Leave this part fluffy.

Add the markings with a mix of black and grey fleece.

girth – 80mm (3 1/4in)

Leave this part fluffy.

Make it thin and solid.

tail (actual size)

Directions:

Make the head, body, legs, and tail with white fleece. Join the parts together.

Mix grey fleece and a small amount of black fleece. Make the ears and attach them to the head.

Use the same mixture and add markings to all parts of the dog.

Attach a black nose to the head.

face (actual size)

▸▸▸p.24/p.38

fleece: Romney (beige, light brown, light grey, reddish brown), merino (black)
weight: approx. 7 grams
glass eyes: 3mm (¹/₈in), medium brown

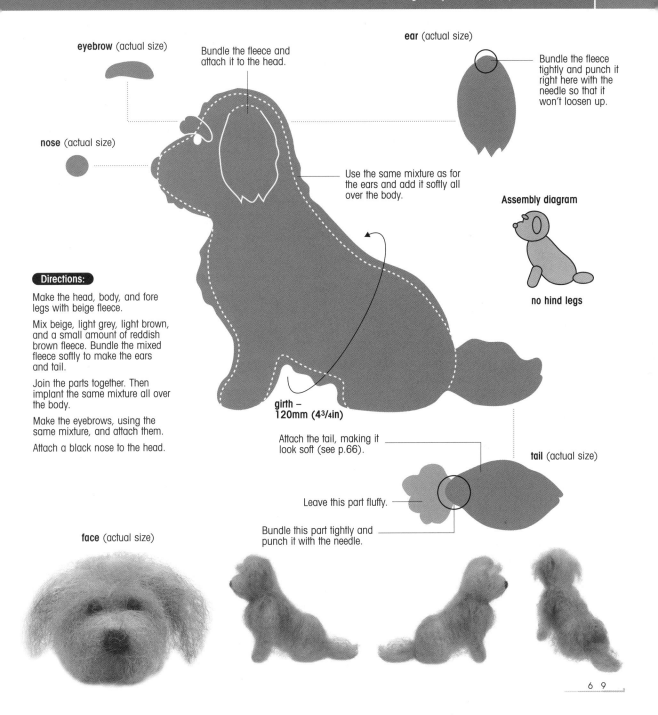

eyebrow (actual size)

Bundle the fleece and attach it to the head.

ear (actual size)

Bundle the fleece tightly and punch it right here with the needle so that it won't loosen up.

nose (actual size)

Use the same mixture as for the ears and add it softly all over the body.

Assembly diagram

no hind legs

Directions:

Make the head, body, and fore legs with beige fleece.

Mix beige, light grey, light brown, and a small amount of reddish brown fleece. Bundle the mixed fleece softly to make the ears and tail.

Join the parts together. Then implant the same mixture all over the body.

Make the eyebrows, using the same mixture, and attach them.

Attach a black nose to the head.

girth –
120mm (4³/₄in)

Attach the tail, making it look soft (see p.66).

tail (actual size)

Leave this part fluffy.

Bundle this part tightly and punch it with the needle.

face (actual size)

13 | Bernese Mountain Dog

fleece: Romney (white, chocolate, reddish brown, black), merino (beige)
weight: approx. 7 grams
glass eyes: 3mm ($^1/_8$in), medium brown

➤➤➤p.25/p.38

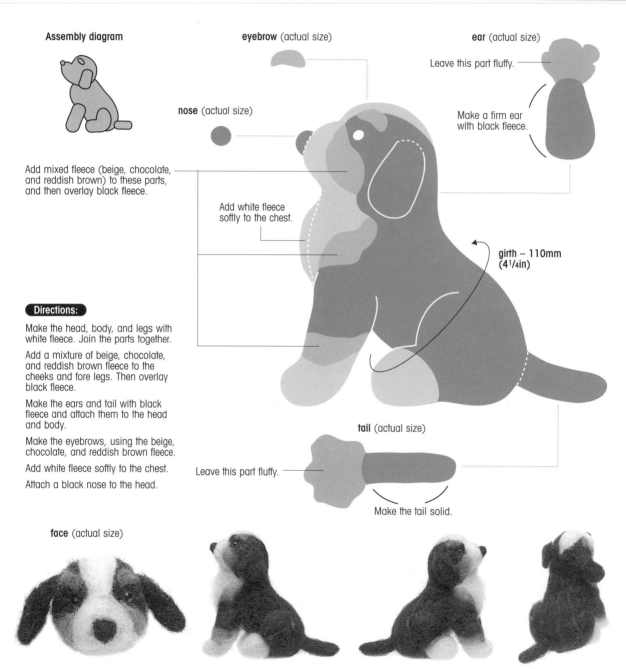

Assembly diagram

eyebrow (actual size)

ear (actual size)

Leave this part fluffy.

Make a firm ear with black fleece.

nose (actual size)

Add mixed fleece (beige, chocolate, and reddish brown) to these parts, and then overlay black fleece.

Add white fleece softly to the chest.

girth – 110mm (4$^1/_4$in)

Directions:

Make the head, body, and legs with white fleece. Join the parts together.

Add a mixture of beige, chocolate, and reddish brown fleece to the cheeks and fore legs. Then overlay black fleece.

Make the ears and tail with black fleece and attach them to the head and body.

Make the eyebrows, using the beige, chocolate, and reddish brown fleece.

Add white fleece softly to the chest.

Attach a black nose to the head.

tail (actual size)

Leave this part fluffy.

Make the tail solid.

face (actual size)

7 0

➤➤➤ p.26/p.38

fleece: Romney (grey, black), alpaca (black)
weight: approx. 5 grams
glass eyes: 2mm (¹/₁₆in), topaz

ear (actual size)

Make this part solid.

Leave this part fluffy.

Assembly diagram

After implanting the eyebrows, and the hair on the muzzle, trim them.

nose (actual size)

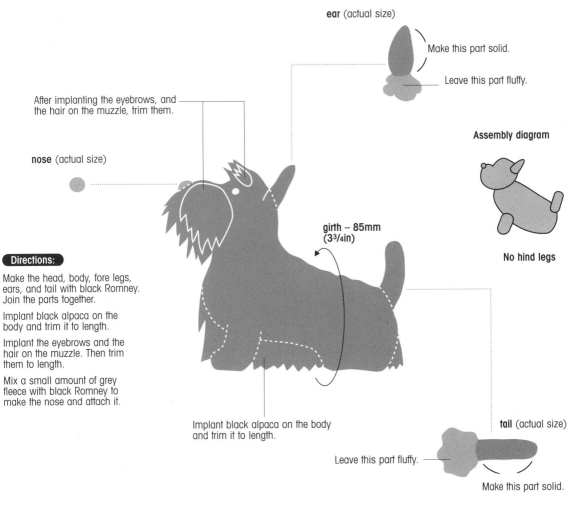

No hind legs

girth – 85mm
(3³/₄in)

Directions:

Make the head, body, fore legs, ears, and tail with black Romney. Join the parts together.

Implant black alpaca on the body and trim it to length.

Implant the eyebrows and the hair on the muzzle. Then trim them to length.

Mix a small amount of grey fleece with black Romney to make the nose and attach it.

Implant black alpaca on the body and trim it to length.

tail (actual size)

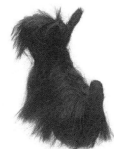

Leave this part fluffy.

Make this part solid.

face (actual size)

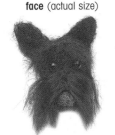

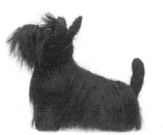

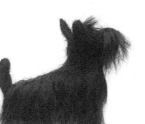

fleece: Romney (white), merino (black), alpaca (white)
weight: approx. 5 grams
glass eyes: 2mm (¹/₁₆in), topaz

➤➤➤p.27/p.39

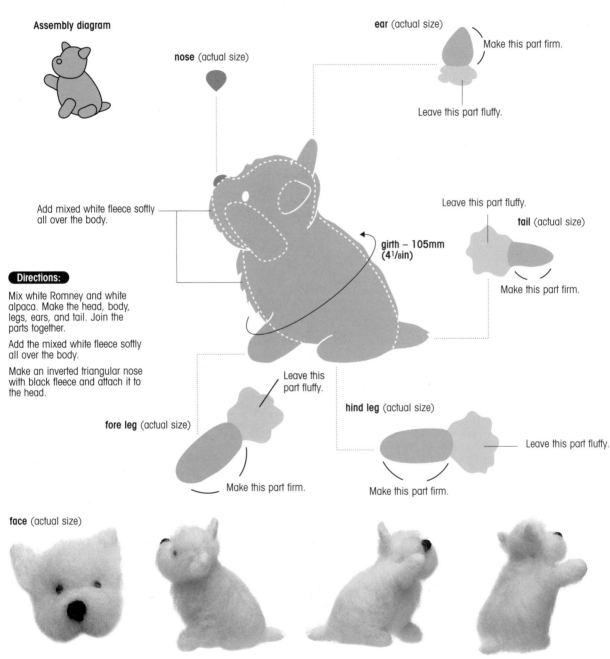

Assembly diagram

nose (actual size)

ear (actual size)

Make this part firm.

Leave this part fluffy.

Add mixed white fleece softly all over the body.

Leave this part fluffy.

tail (actual size)

girth – 105mm (4¹/₈in)

Make this part firm.

Directions:

Mix white Romney and white alpaca. Make the head, body, legs, ears, and tail. Join the parts together.

Add the mixed white fleece softly all over the body.

Make an inverted triangular nose with black fleece and attach it to the head.

Leave this part fluffy.

hind leg (actual size)

fore leg (actual size)

Leave this part fluffy.

Make this part firm.

Make this part firm.

face (actual size)

➡➡p.28/p.39

fleece: Romney (chocolate), merino (black, dark grey) alpaca (dark brown)
weight: approx. 8 grams
glass eyes: 3mm (¹/₈in), medium brown

Directions:

Make the head, body, legs, and tail with a mixture of chocolate and dark grey fleece. Join the parts together.

Randomly mix all the colours of fleece, except chocolate. Implant the mixture, without blending it, on the body in a few stages to make tiers.

Implant tiers of fleece on the ears in the same way as for the body. Trim them to shape, checking the overall balance.

Make the nose with black merino and attach it to the head.

nose (actual size)

tail (actual size)

Leave this part fluffy.

Make this part solid.

Implant the ears here.

girth – 120mm (4³/₄in)

fore leg (actual size)

Leave this part fluffy.

Make this part solid.

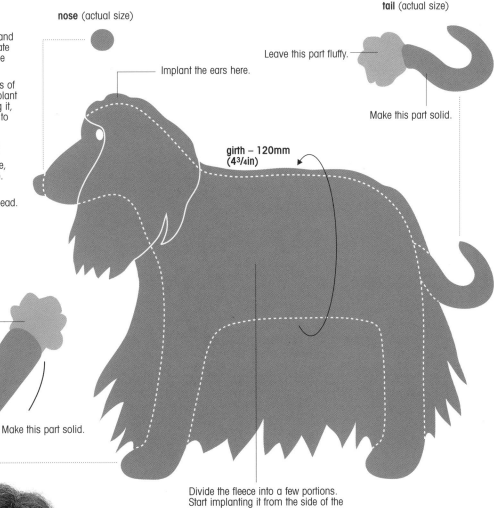

face (actual size)

Divide the fleece into a few portions. Start implanting it from the side of the abdomen and work up to make tiers.

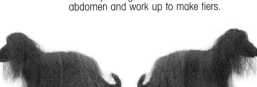

fleece: Romney (black), Gotland (black)
weight: approx. 16 grams
glass eyes: 6mm (¼in), clear

➤➤➤ p.29/p.39

nose (actual size)

Make the forehead slightly prominent.

Assembly diagram

Lightly add Gotland fleece all over.

Directions:

Make the head, body, legs, and tail with black Romney. Then join the parts together.

Put a thin layer of Gotland fleece all over the body, handling the fleece carefully so that it doesn't lose its curl.

Make the ears with Gotland fleece and set them slightly low.

Make the forehead slightly prominent.

Make the nose with black Romney and attach it to the head.

Attach the glass eyes with thread (see p.61).

ear (actual size)

Leave this part fluffy.

Make this part firm.

tail (actual size)

Make this part solid.

fore leg (actual size)

Make this part solid.

Leave this part fluffy.

girth – 145mm (5¾in)

Leave this part fluffy.

face (actual size)

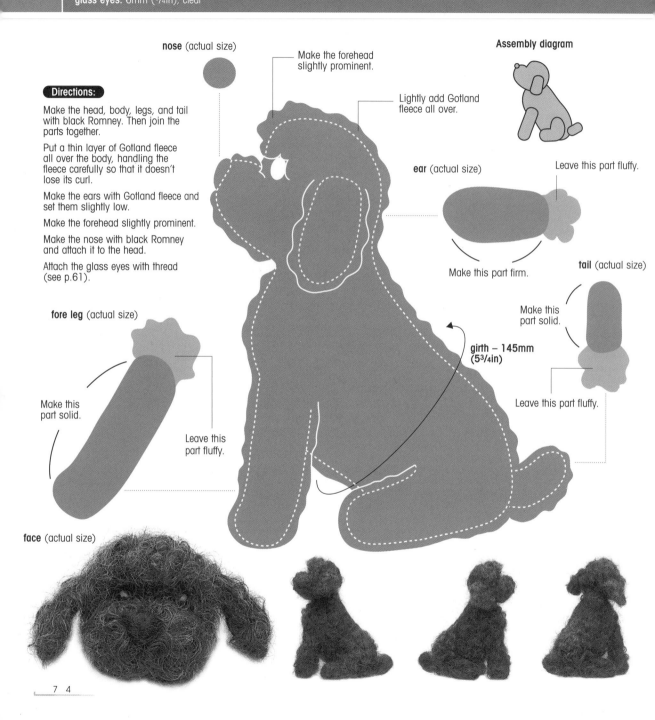

▸▸▸ p.42

fleece: Romney (light grey, beige), merino (black, white), dog hair
weight: approx. 7 grams
glass eyes: 3mm (1/8in), medium brown

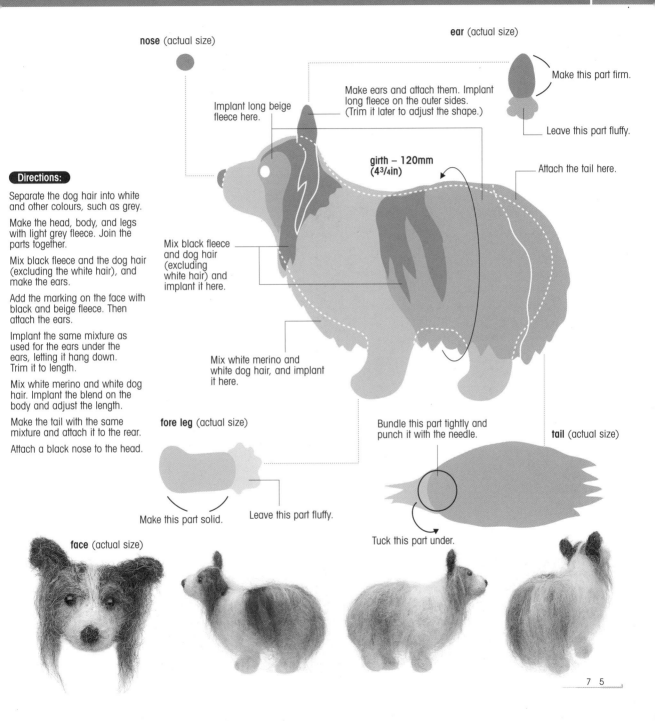

nose (actual size)

ear (actual size)

Implant long beige fleece here.

Make ears and attach them. Implant long fleece on the outer sides. (Trim it later to adjust the shape.)

Make this part firm.

Leave this part fluffy.

girth – 120mm (4³/₄in)

Attach the tail here.

Mix black fleece and dog hair (excluding white hair) and implant it here.

Mix white merino and white dog hair, and implant it here.

Directions:

Separate the dog hair into white and other colours, such as grey.

Make the head, body, and legs with light grey fleece. Join the parts together.

Mix black fleece and the dog hair (excluding the white hair), and make the ears.

Add the marking on the face with black and beige fleece. Then attach the ears.

Implant the same mixture as used for the ears under the ears, letting it hang down. Trim it to length.

Mix white merino and white dog hair. Implant the blend on the body and adjust the length.

Make the tail with the same mixture and attach it to the rear.

Attach a black nose to the head.

fore leg (actual size)

Make this part solid.

Leave this part fluffy.

Bundle this part tightly and punch it with the needle.

tail (actual size)

Tuck this part under.

face (actual size)

fleece: Romney (white, chocolate, beige), merino (black), alpaca (brown), mohair (white), dog hair
weight: approx. 7 grams
glass eyes: 3mm (1/8in), medium brown

➤➤➤ p.44

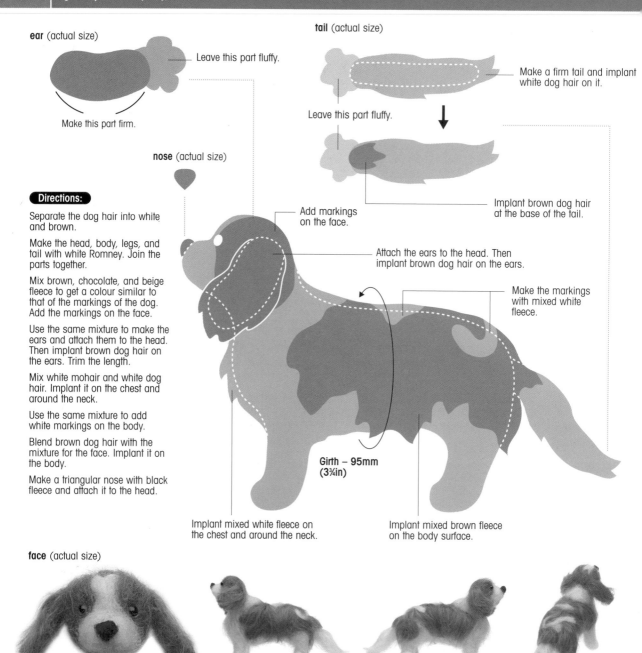

ear (actual size)

Leave this part fluffy.

Make this part firm.

nose (actual size)

tail (actual size)

Make a firm tail and implant white dog hair on it.

Leave this part fluffy.

Implant brown dog hair at the base of the tail.

Add markings on the face.

Attach the ears to the head. Then implant brown dog hair on the ears.

Make the markings with mixed white fleece.

Directions:

Separate the dog hair into white and brown.

Make the head, body, legs, and tail with white Romney. Join the parts together.

Mix brown, chocolate, and beige fleece to get a colour similar to that of the markings of the dog. Add the markings on the face.

Use the same mixture to make the ears and attach them to the head. Then implant brown dog hair on the ears. Trim the length.

Mix white mohair and white dog hair. Implant it on the chest and around the neck.

Use the same mixture to add white markings on the body.

Blend brown dog hair with the mixture for the face. Implant it on the body.

Make a triangular nose with black fleece and attach it to the head.

Girth – 95mm (3¾in)

Implant mixed white fleece on the chest and around the neck.

Implant mixed brown fleece on the body surface.

face (actual size)

▸▸▸p.46 **fleece:** Romney (light grey, dark brown, chocolate), merino (black, white, greyish brown, medium grey), dog hair
weight: approx. 7 grams
glass eyes: 3mm (¹/₈in), medium brown

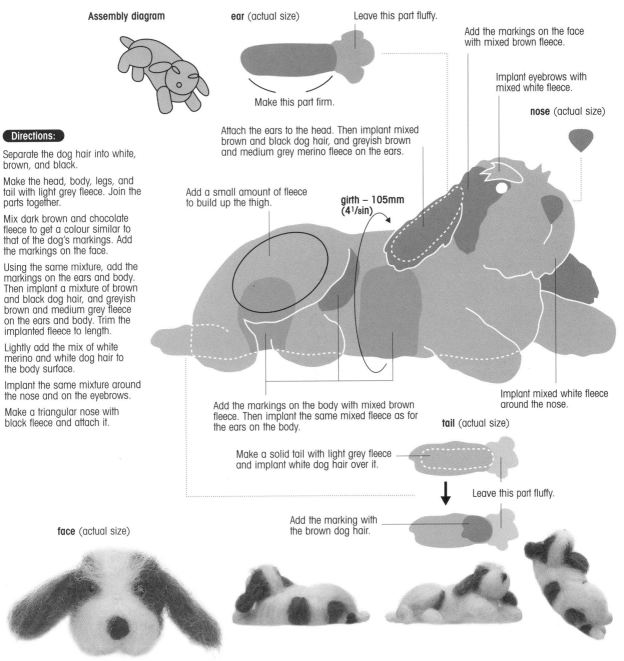

Assembly diagram

ear (actual size)

Leave this part fluffy.

Make this part firm.

Add the markings on the face with mixed brown fleece.

Implant eyebrows with mixed white fleece.

nose (actual size)

Attach the ears to the head. Then implant mixed brown and black dog hair, and greyish brown and medium grey merino fleece on the ears.

Add a small amount of fleece to build up the thigh.

girth – 105mm (4¹/₈in)

Directions:

Separate the dog hair into white, brown, and black.

Make the head, body, legs, and tail with light grey fleece. Join the parts together.

Mix dark brown and chocolate fleece to get a colour similar to that of the dog's markings. Add the markings on the face.

Using the same mixture, add the markings on the ears and body. Then implant a mixture of brown and black dog hair, and greyish brown and medium grey fleece on the ears and body. Trim the implanted fleece to length.

Lightly add the mix of white merino and white dog hair to the body surface.

Implant the same mixture around the nose and on the eyebrows.

Make a triangular nose with black fleece and attach it.

Implant mixed white fleece around the nose.

Add the markings on the body with mixed brown fleece. Then implant the same mixed fleece as for the ears on the body.

tail (actual size)

Make a solid tail with light grey fleece and implant white dog hair over it.

Leave this part fluffy.

Add the marking with the brown dog hair.

face (actual size)

How to Make a Frame

I will now show you how to make a frame for the body. Although a frame is optional, you will find it adds stability to the body and makes work easier.

Also, it will allow you to pose your finished pieces the way you like.

Things you need

2 pieces of aluminium wire (20cm (8in) long; 1–2mm (1/16in) diameter)
4 pieces of spindle cord 1cm (3/8in) longer than the leg
scissors, pliers

Making a frame

01 Take two pieces of wire. Twist them together, intertwining 5cm (2in) in the middle. Twist more or less than this, depending on the size of the dog you are making.

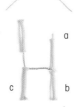

02 Make an "H" shape with the wire and thread it into a piece of spindle cord (a), cut the wire sticking out of the string (b), and fold back about 5mm (1/4in) at the end (c). Repeat the process for the three other pieces of wire.

a

b

c

Adding fleece to the legs

03 On a needle cushion, roll fleece around each leg (see p.51).

Standing the frame up

04 After adding fleece to the legs, bend the two pieces of wire to make two "U"-shapes and stand the frame up. (If the lengths of the legs are not the same, add a small amount of fleece to the paw of the short leg.)

Adding fleece to the body

05 Roll 1/2 gram of fleece tightly around the wire (see p.52). This will be the core of the body.

06 Add another 1/2 gram of fleece around the frame, covering the body.

07 Punch the fleece on the body evenly with the needle. Check the proportion of the legs to the body and adjust the shape.

After this, follow the steps starting at step 13 on p.53.

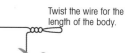

Rough guide to the lengths of wire frame for each dog

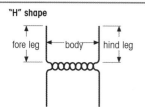

"H" shape

fore leg — body — hind leg

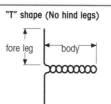

"T" shape (No hind legs)

fore leg — body

How to make a "T" shape frame

Prepare a piece of wire that is a little longer than you need. Bend it in half. ➡

Twist the wire for the length of the body.

Bend it into a "T" shape and cut the wire, leaving the lengths of the fore legs.

Breed	Shape	Fore legs	Body	Hind legs
01 Labrador Retriever	H	5.5 (2 1/8)	5 (2)	5.5 (2 1/8)
02 Miniature Dachshund	H	3.5 (1 3/8)	4 (1 1/2)	3.5 (1 3/8)
03 Shiba Inu	H	5 (2)	4.5 (1 3/4)	5 (2)
04 French Bulldog	H	4.5 (1 3/4)	4 (1 1/2)	4.5 (1 3/4)
05 Wirehaired Fox Terrier	H	6 (2 1/4)	4.5 (1 3/4)	6 (2 1/4)
06 Siberian Husky	H	5.5 (2 1/8)	5 (2)	5.5 (2 1/8)
07 Chihuahua	H	3.5 (1 3/8)	3 (1 1/8)	3.5 (1 3/8)
08 Miniature Schnauzer	H	5.5 (2 1/8)	4.5 (1 3/4)	3.5 (1 3/8)
09 Pomeranian	H	4.5 (1 3/4)	4 (1 1/2)	4.5 (1 3/4)
10 Papillon	H	4.5 (1 3/4)	4 (1 1/2)	4.5 (1 3/4)

Breed	Shape	Fore legs	Body	Hind legs
11 Dalmatian	H	5.5 (2 1/8)	4 (1 1/2)	5.5 (2 1/8)
12 Catalan Sheepdog	T	5.5 (2 1/8)	5 (2)	N/A
13 Bernese Mountain Dog	H	5.5 (2 1/8)	5 (2)	3.5 (1 3/8)
14 Scottish Terrier	T	3 (1 1/8)	4 (1 1/2)	N/A
15 West Highland White Terrier	H	4.5 (1 3/4)	4 (1 1/2)	3 (1 1/8)
16 Afghan Hound	H	7 (2 3/4)	5.5 (2 1/8)	7 (2 3/4)
17 Toy Poodle	H	8 (3 1/4)	7 (2 3/4)	5 (2)
18 Shetland Sheepdog	H	5 (2)	4.5 (1 3/4)	5 (2)
19 Cavalier King Charles Spaniel	H	5 (2)	5 (2)	5 (2)
20 Petit Basset Griffon Vendeen	H	5 (2)	5 (2)	5 (2)

Lengths are given in cm (in), with a margin of 0.5cm (1/4in) on the fore leg and hind leg for folding.

Mail Order Kits

Fleece Dog kits are available via mail order.

Each kit contains fleece, one needle, materials for a frame, and glass eyes for a specific breed.

Scissors and pliers are not included.

Kits are available for Fleece Dogs Nos. 01 to 17 in this book.

Bone-shaped needle cushions, which are useful for making parts, are also available.

As some of the kits are in limited supply, they may not be available.

For the latest information on Fleece Dog kits and other products, please visit SINCO's website **www.fleecedog.com**

How to order

Purchase online or send a fax if you don't use the Internet.
Fax number is +81 (0)45-561-2191. (This is a Japanese number.)

Shipping and handling

Shipping and handling charges are based on the geographic area of the destination. The kits will be shipped from Japan.

Payment

We accept payment by credit card only (Visa, MasterCard, UC, JCB, NIKOS, American Express and Diners Club International).

Contact Information

SINCO Fleece Dog Kit
Fax: +81 (0)45-561-2191. (This is a Japanese number.)
Email: mail@fleecedog.com

Note

Due to reproduction and printing, the colours of the fleece in this book may not be exactly the same as the actual colours supplied in the kits.

Mail Order Supplies

The following companies offer a range of needle felting supplies. Felting needles are very sharp and quite fragile. They are available in packs, so you may like to order more than one and keep a supply handy.

Felting and Needle Felting Forum
http://feltingforum.com
Online forum for discussing felting and needle felting

UK

Woodland Teddies; **www.woodlandteddies.com** Sells: felting needles, starter kits, foam blocks, and other supplies

Christie Bears; **www.christiebears.co.uk** Sells: felting needles, fleece, foam block

Threshing Barn; **www.threshingbarn.com** Sells: felting needles, fleece, and other supplies

Rainbow Silks; **www.rainbowsilks.co.uk**
Email:caroline@rainbowsilks.co.uk Sells: felting needles, felting mats

Felt Head to Toe; **www.feltheadtotoe.co.uk** Sells: felting needles and other supplies

Knitshop; **www.knitshop.co.uk** Sells: felting needles, fleece, and other supplies

Scottish Fibres; **www.scottishfibres.co.uk** Email: enquiries@scottishfibres.co.uk Sells: felting needles

USA

Earthsong Fibers; **www.earthsongfibers.com** Email: esf@earthsongfibers.com Sells: felting needles, needle felting starter kits, felting fleece packs

Pacific Wool and Fiber; **www.pacificwoolandfiber.com** Sells: needles, fibre, and other supplies

Halcyon Yarn; **www.halcyonyarn.com** Email: service@halcyonyarn.net Sells: Felting needles, fibre, felting blocks

The Woolery; **www.woolery.com** Sells: felting needles, fibre, kits, books

The Wool Shed; Email: woolshed@juno.com Sells: felting needles, fibre

Mielke's Fiber Arts; **www.mielkesfarm.com** Sells: felting needles, fibre, and other supplies

Joggles.com; **www.joggles.com** Sells: felting needles, fleece, and other supplies

The Felted Ewe; **myndzi.tripod.com/thefeltedewe** Sells: all kinds of needle felting supplies

Living Felt; **www.livingfelt.com** Sells: needles and foam pads

Yarnies; **www.yarnies.com** Sells: needle felting supplies

Weir Dolls & Crafts; **www.weirdollsandcrafts.com** Email: info@weirdollsandcrafts.com Sells: felting needles, fleece, foam, kits

AUSTRALIA

www.bearycheap.com Sells: felting needles, wool fibre, foam blocks, beginner's packs

Needlefelting.com; **www.needlefelting.com** Email: rita@needlefelting.com Sells: needles, fibre, and accessories

Sources of suppliers and equipment for feltmaking
www.peak.org/~spark/feltsources

Profile

SINCO (Nobuko Nagakubo)

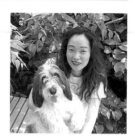

Nobuko Nagakubo, a.k.a. SINCO, studied at Blooming Affairs, a florist's in Boston, USA. On returning to Japan, she founded NON'S TOPIARY. She designs animal-shaped topiaries and holds private exhibitions.

When she learned how to make felt with a "magic needle," she started creating miniature dogs using wool and dog hair. After publishing **Fleece Dog** in Japan in 2004, she began using the name SINCO. She holds workshops and is very popular with dog lovers in Japan. Her dog, CJ, is a Petit Basset Griffon Vendeen.

TAKUMI SATOH

Takumi Satoh studied at Chelsea College of Art & Design in London, England. After returning to Japan, he specialized in using Mac computers at Tokyo Design Academy. He is a graphic designer for an advertising agency, and runs Satoh Color Co. Ltd. with his wife, Yasuka, specializing in designing books and t-shirts, and producing picture books.

YASUKA SATOH

Yasuka Satoh studied plastic art at the Joshibi University of Art and Design, then worked as an illustrator and designer for an advertising agency. She is now in charge of illustrations at Satoh Color Co. Ltd.

YASUO NAGUMO

Yasuo Nagumo was born in 1961. He graduated from the Department of Photography, College of Art, Nihon University. His distinctive style of photography, which has a translucent quality, has made him popular in the field of magazines and books on handicrafts and cookery. He has worked on numerous books for famous writers and chefs. He lives in Tokyo. His pet dog is a Miniature Schnauzer.

ACKNOWLEDGMENTS

SPECIAL THANKS TO
Mr. and Mrs. Satoh, Mrs. Azusa Kaneyasu, Ms. Isako Shirae, and all of you who always cheer me up on the work front and took part in distributing this book. Thank you all!

Fleece Dog
A little bit of magic created with raw wool and a special needle
by SINCO

First published in Great Britain in 2006 by Mitchell Beazley, an imprint of Octopus Publishing Group Limited, 2–4 Heron Quays, London E14 4JP.
Originally published by Bunka Publishing Bureau, 3-22-7 Yoyogi, Shibuya-ku, Tokyo 151-8524, Japan

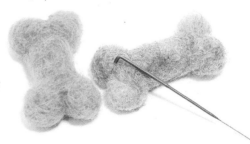

ISBN-13: 978 1 84533 289 1
ISBN-10: 1 84533 289 X

Design: Takumi Satoh (SATOH COLOR)
Illustration: Yasuka Satoh (SATOH COLOR)
Photography: Yasuo Nagumo

Set in typeface Avant Garde Lt

Colour reproduction by Sang Choy, Singapore
Printed and bound in China .

> **Warning:** The miniatures shown are not toys and should not be given to babies or young children.
>
> Felting needles have tiny barbs, so take care not to injure your fingers with them.